Unicorn coloring Book for Kids ages 5-8

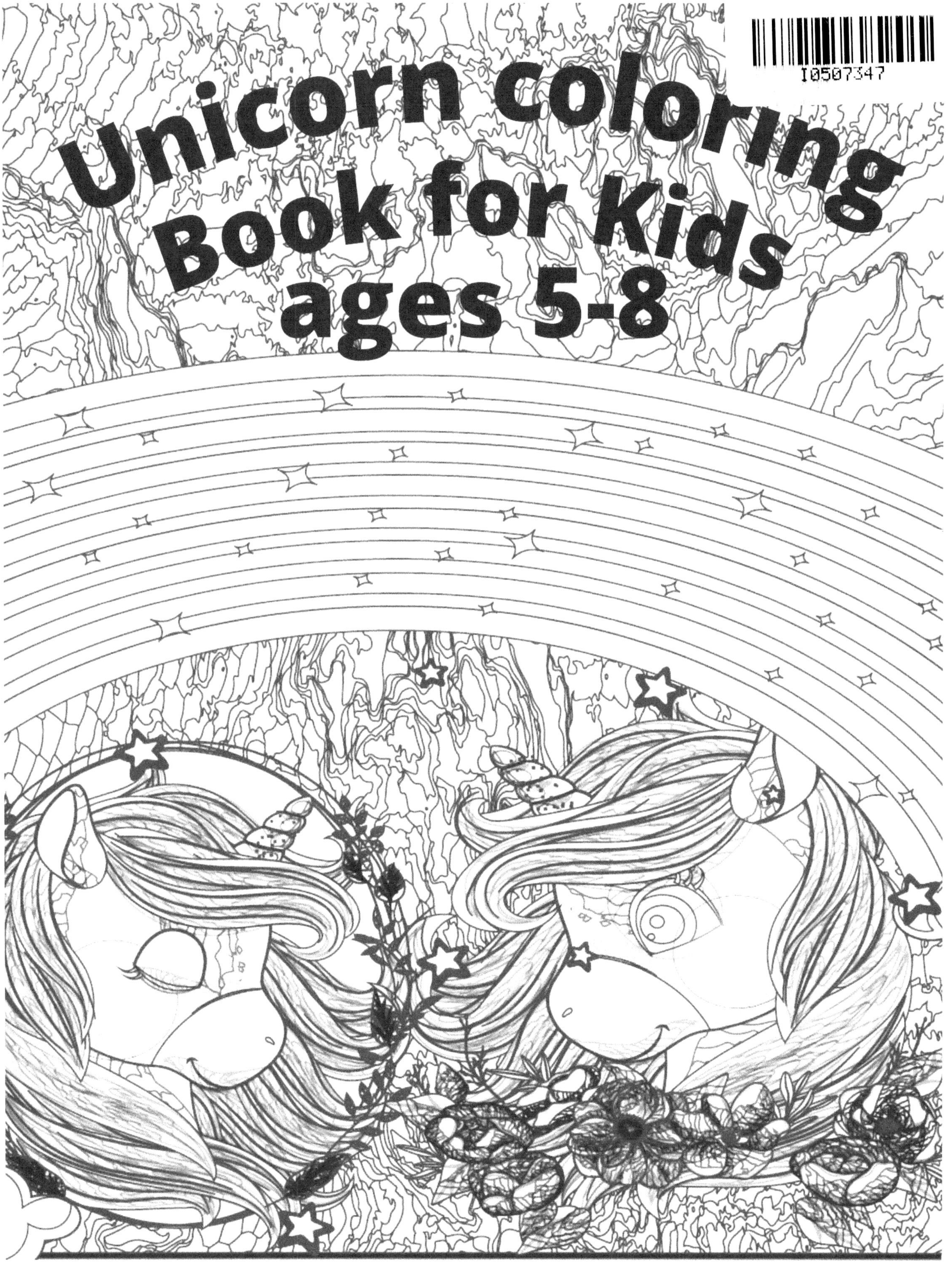

THIS BOOK BELONGS TO

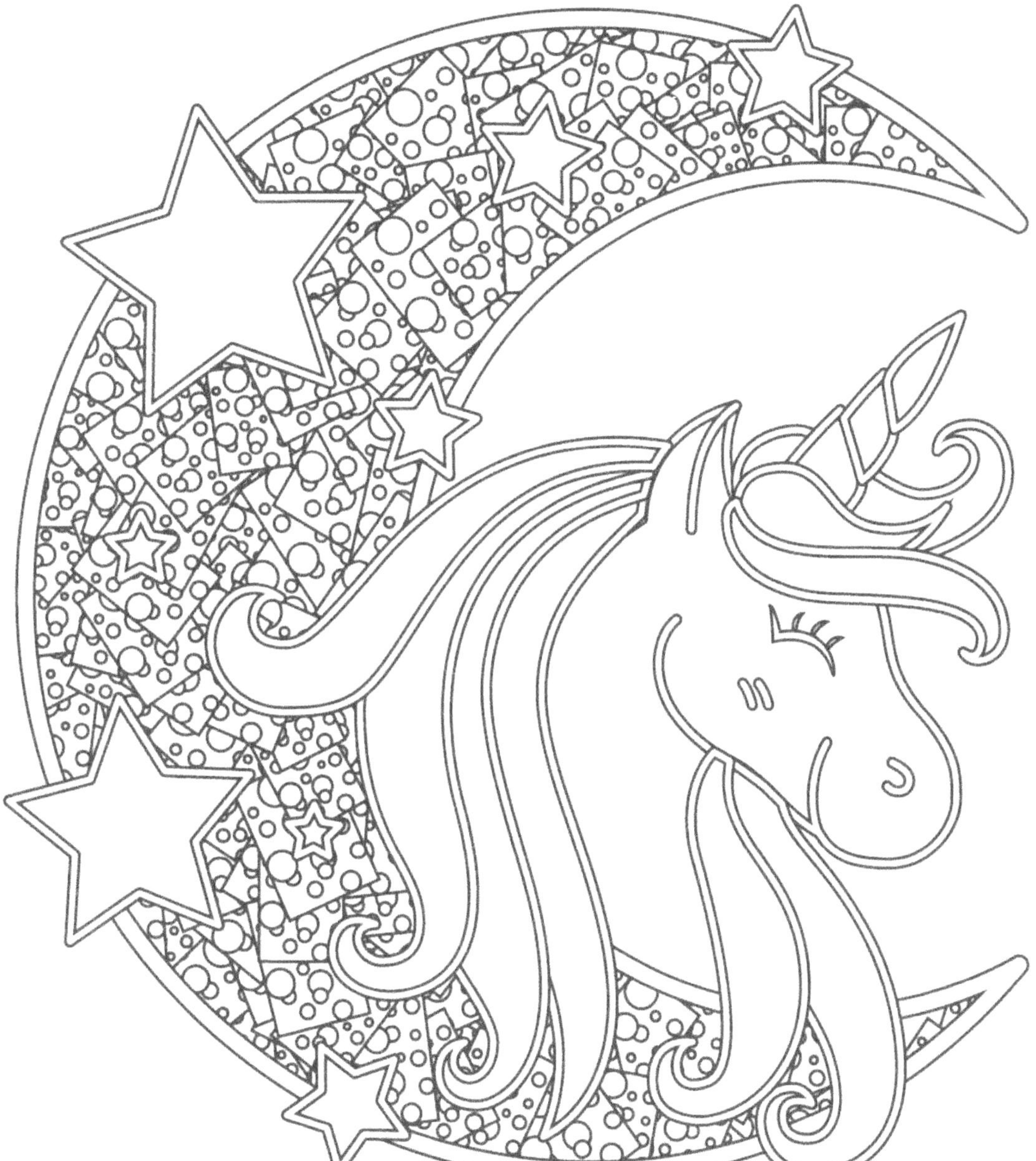

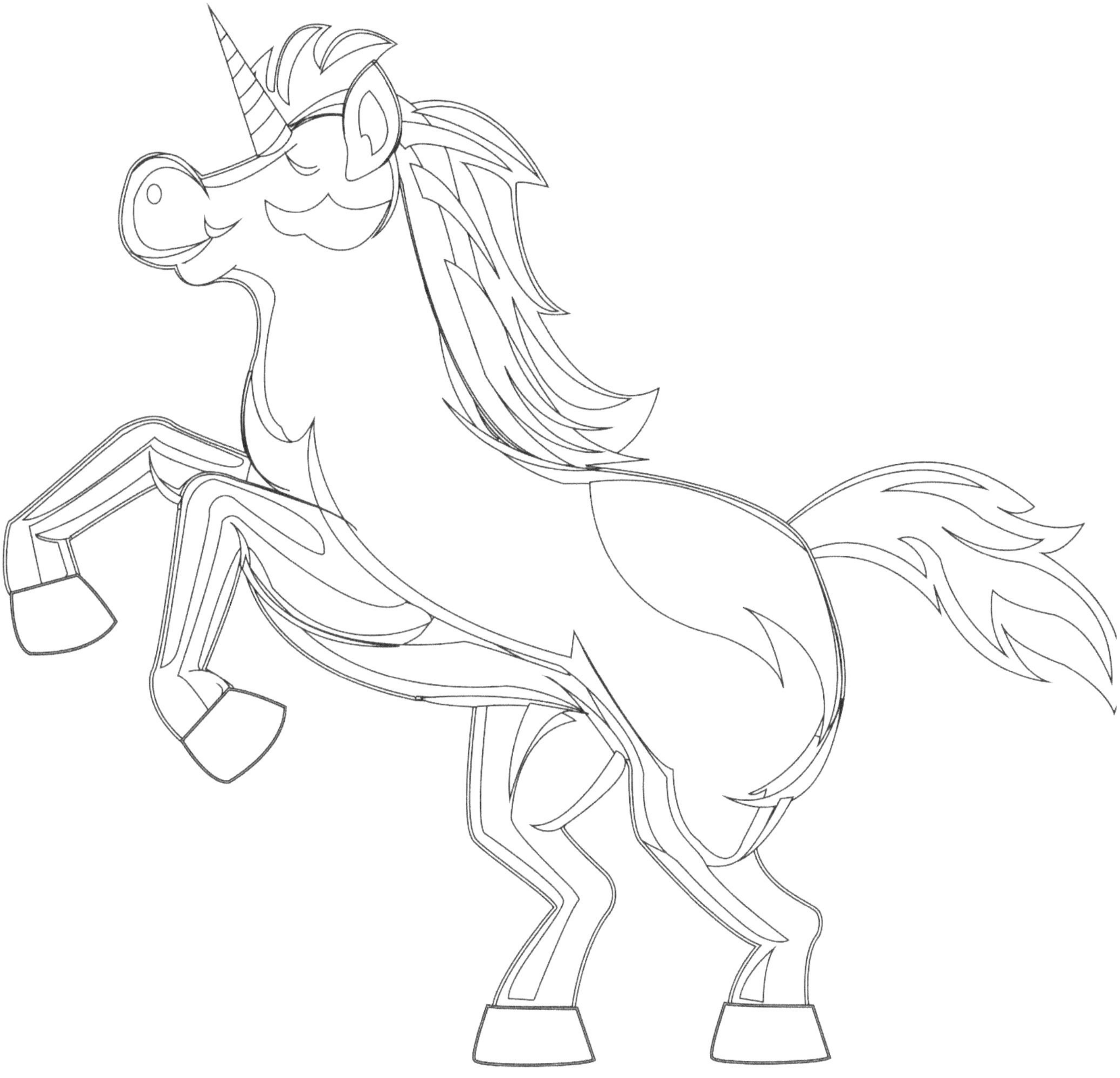

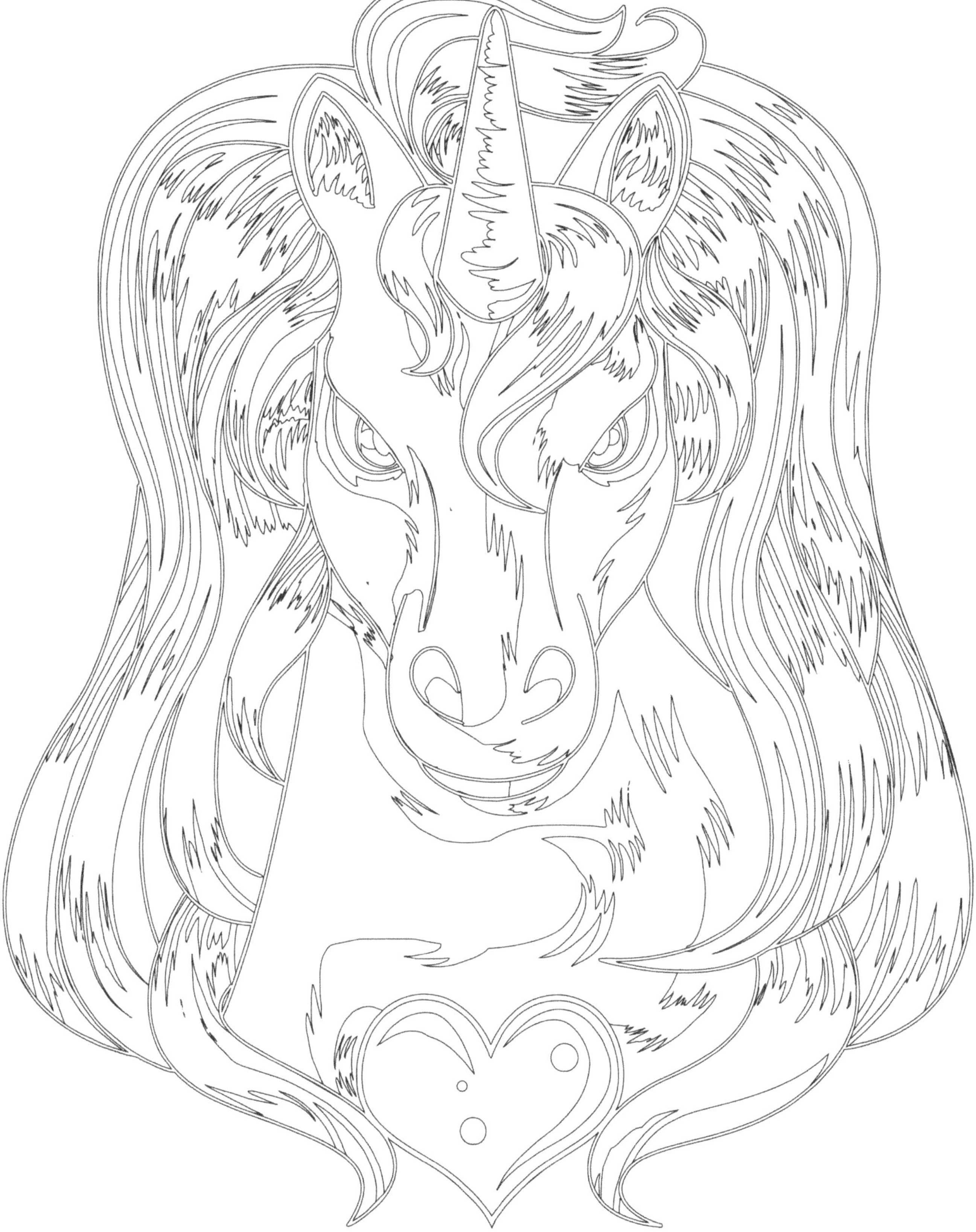

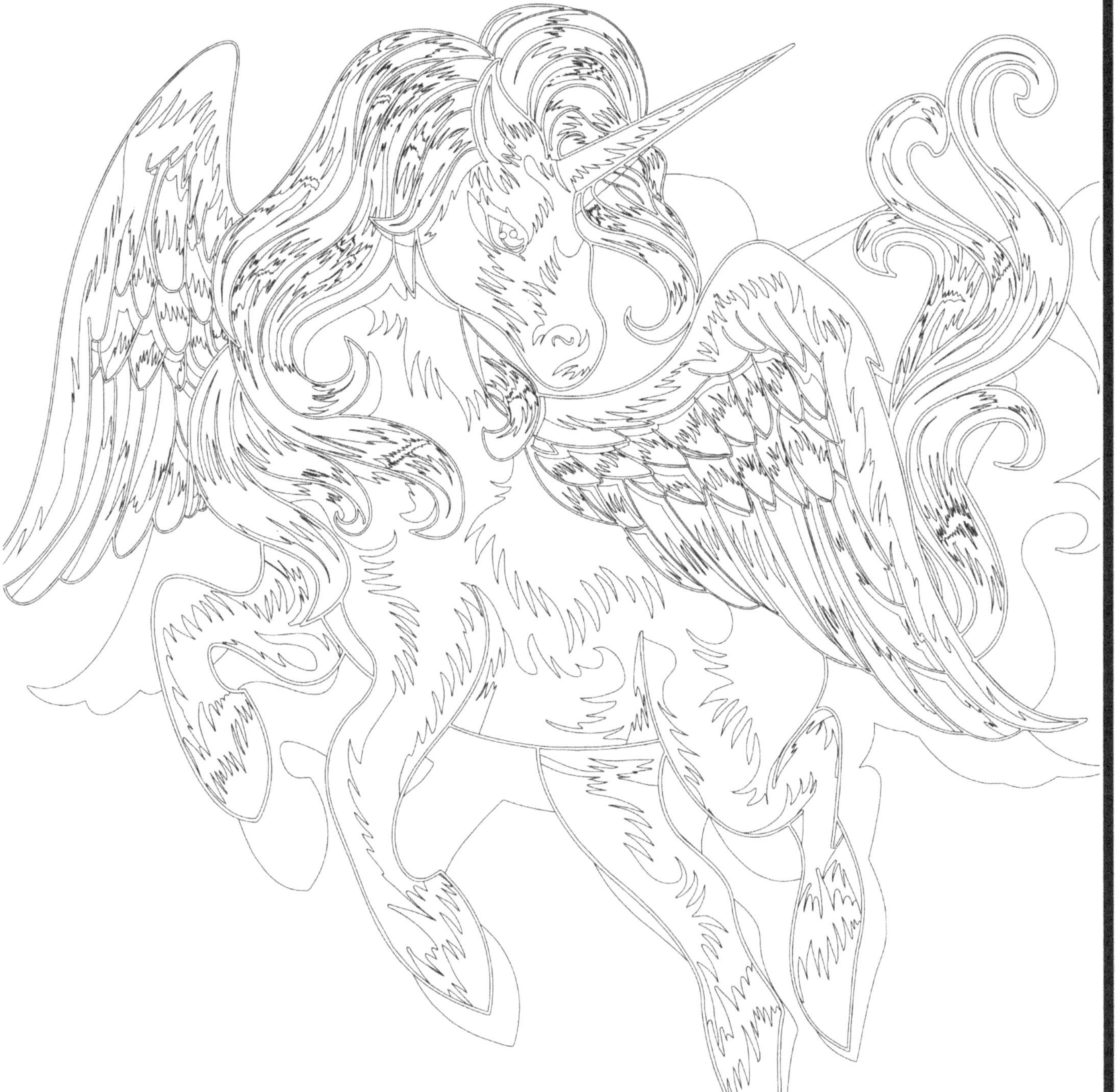

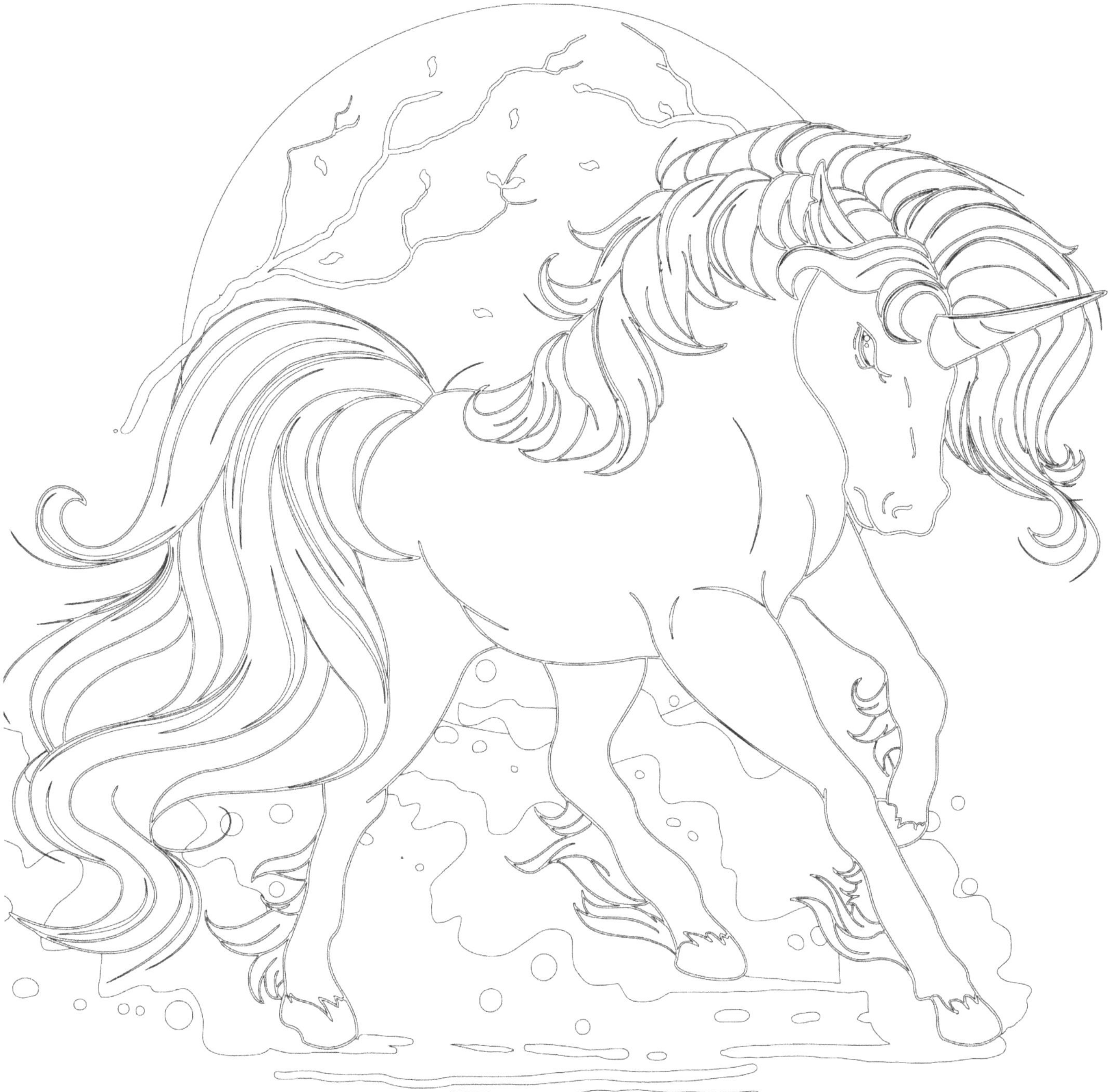

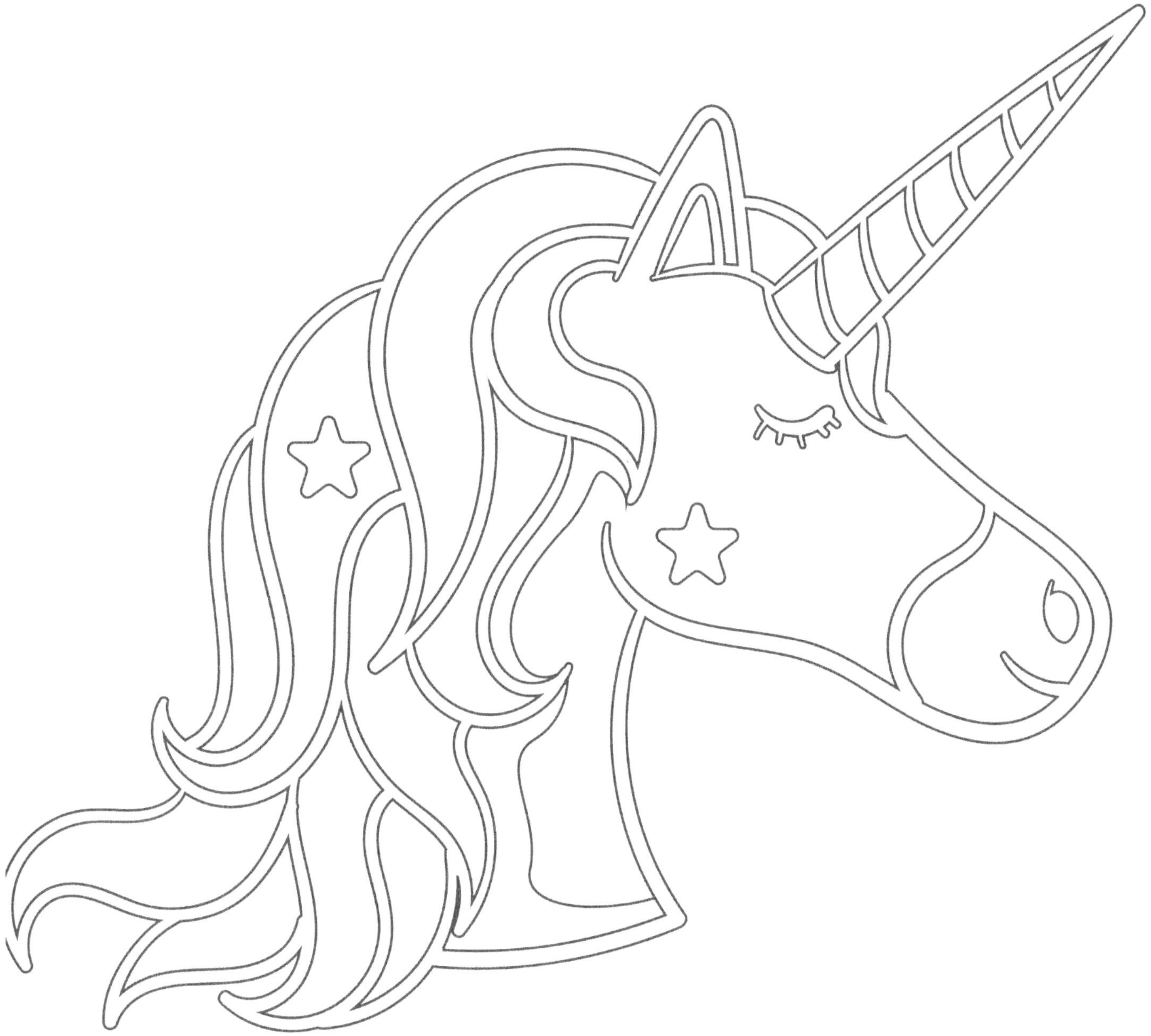

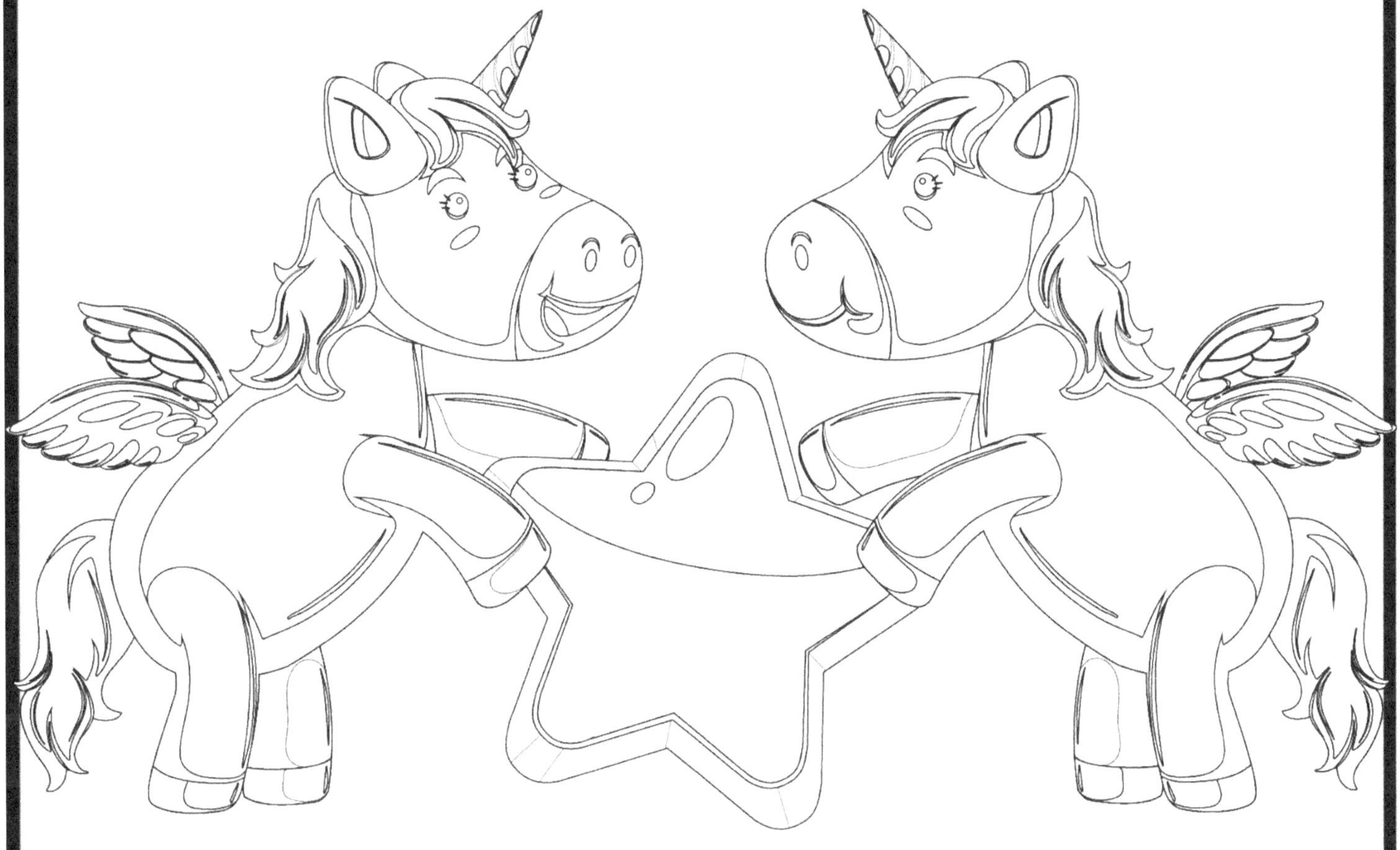

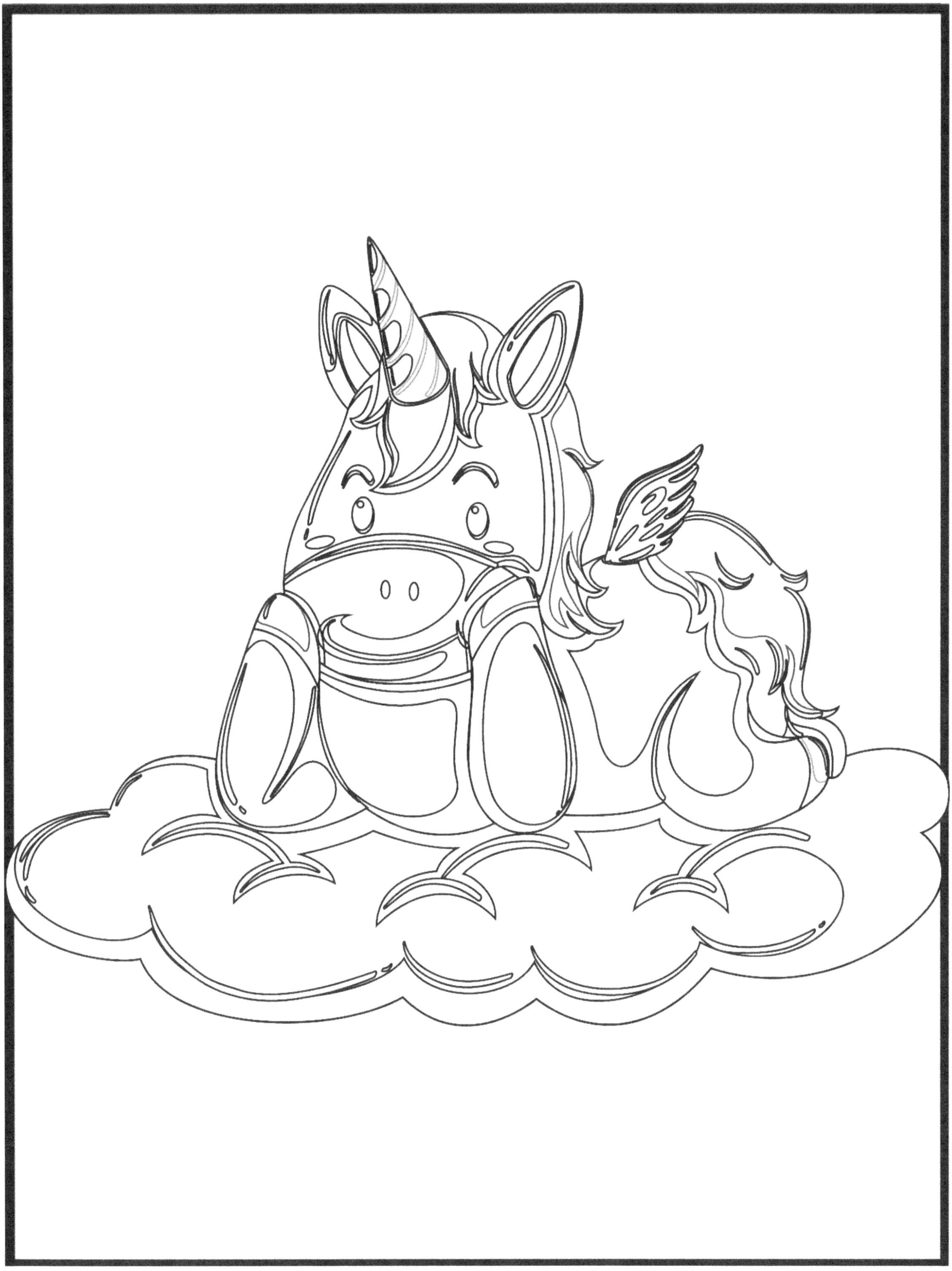

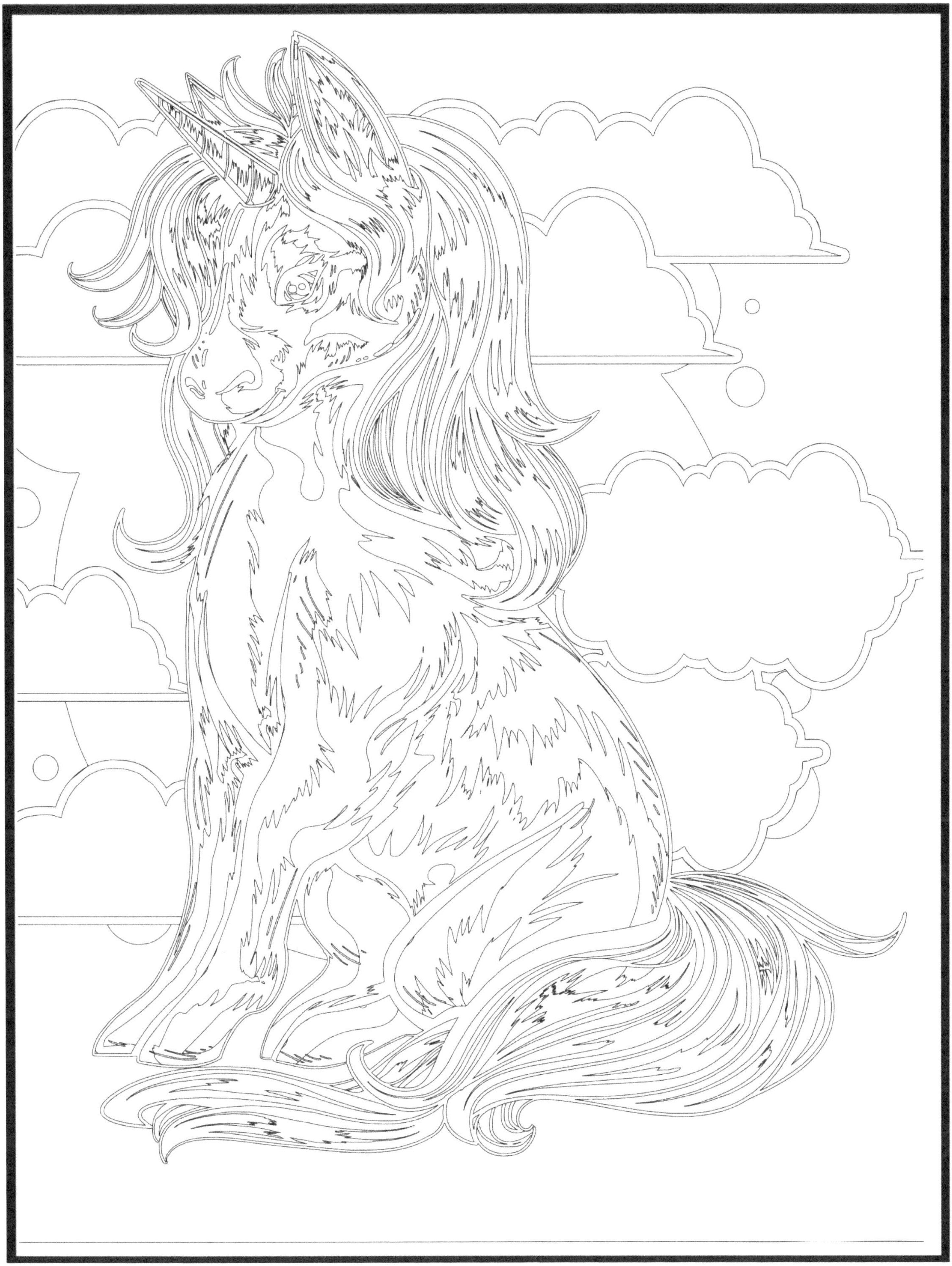

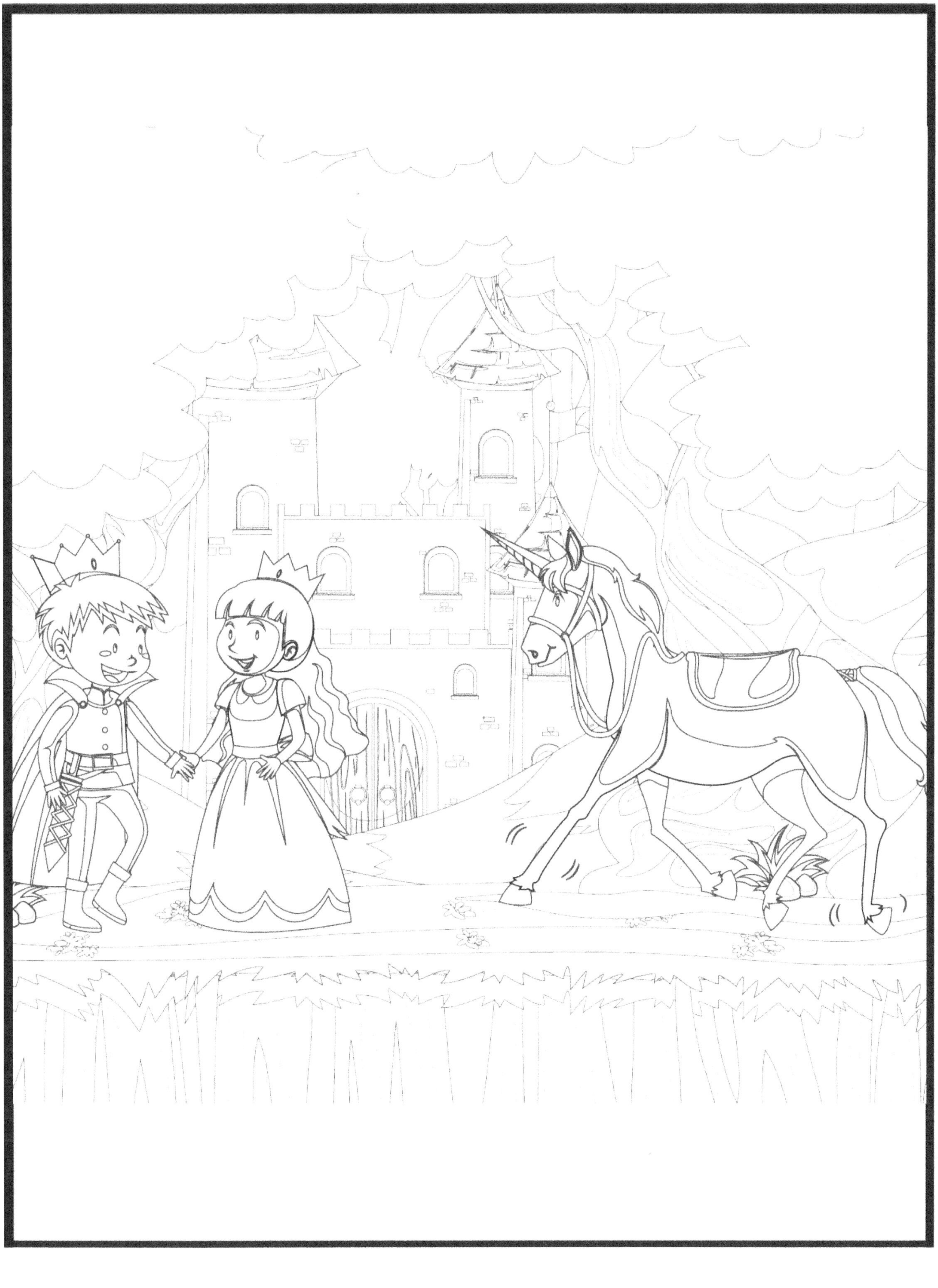

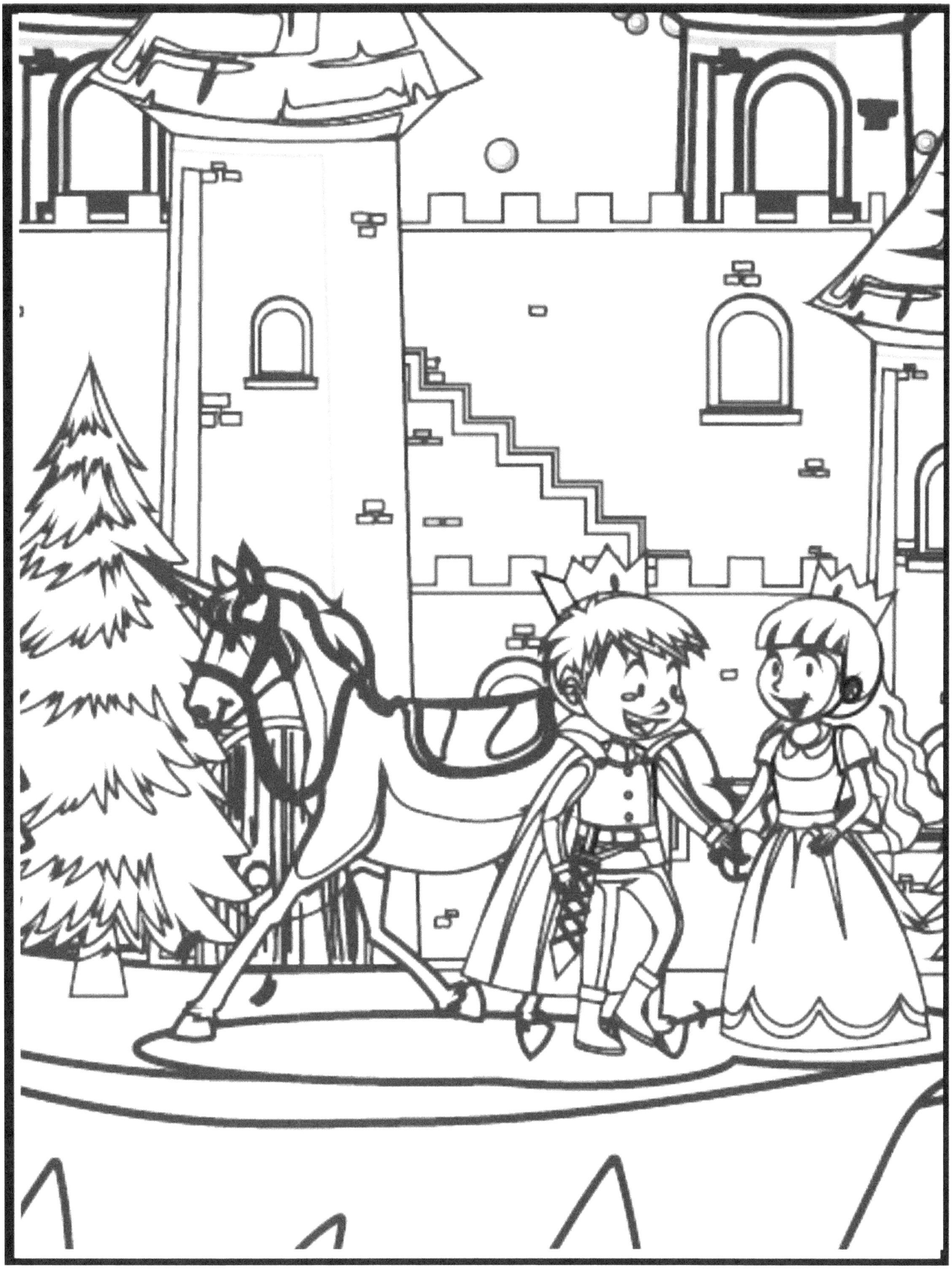

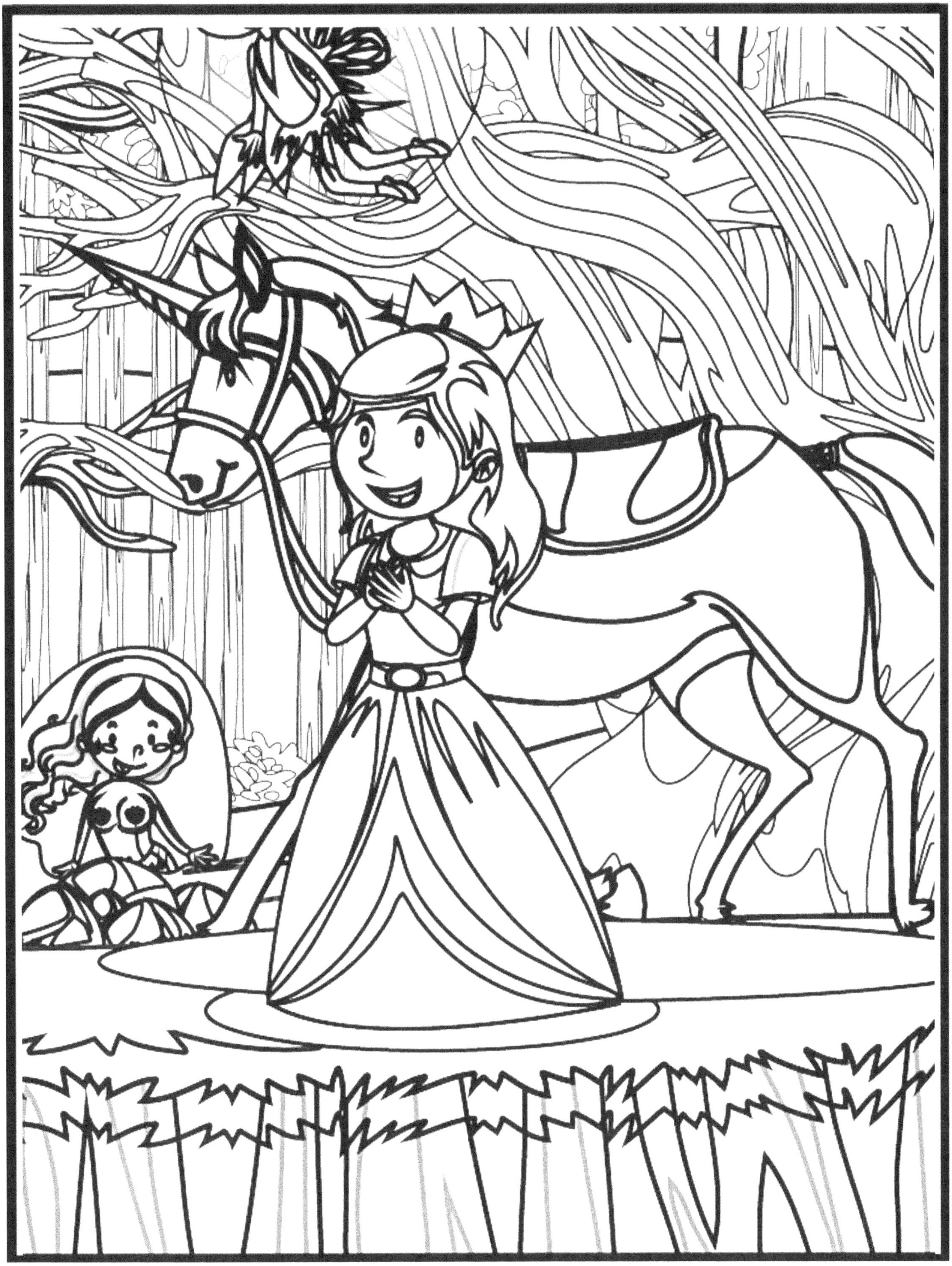

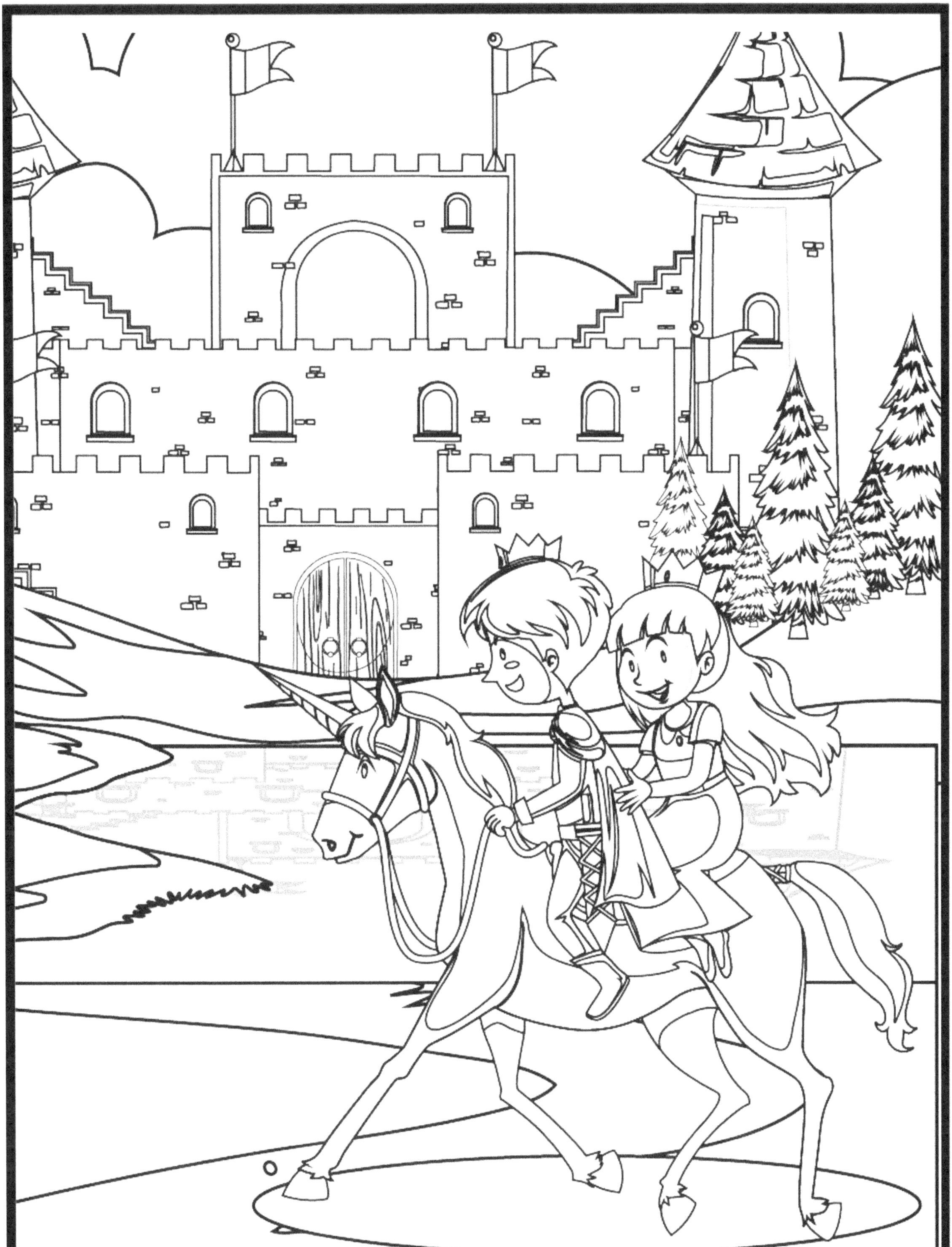

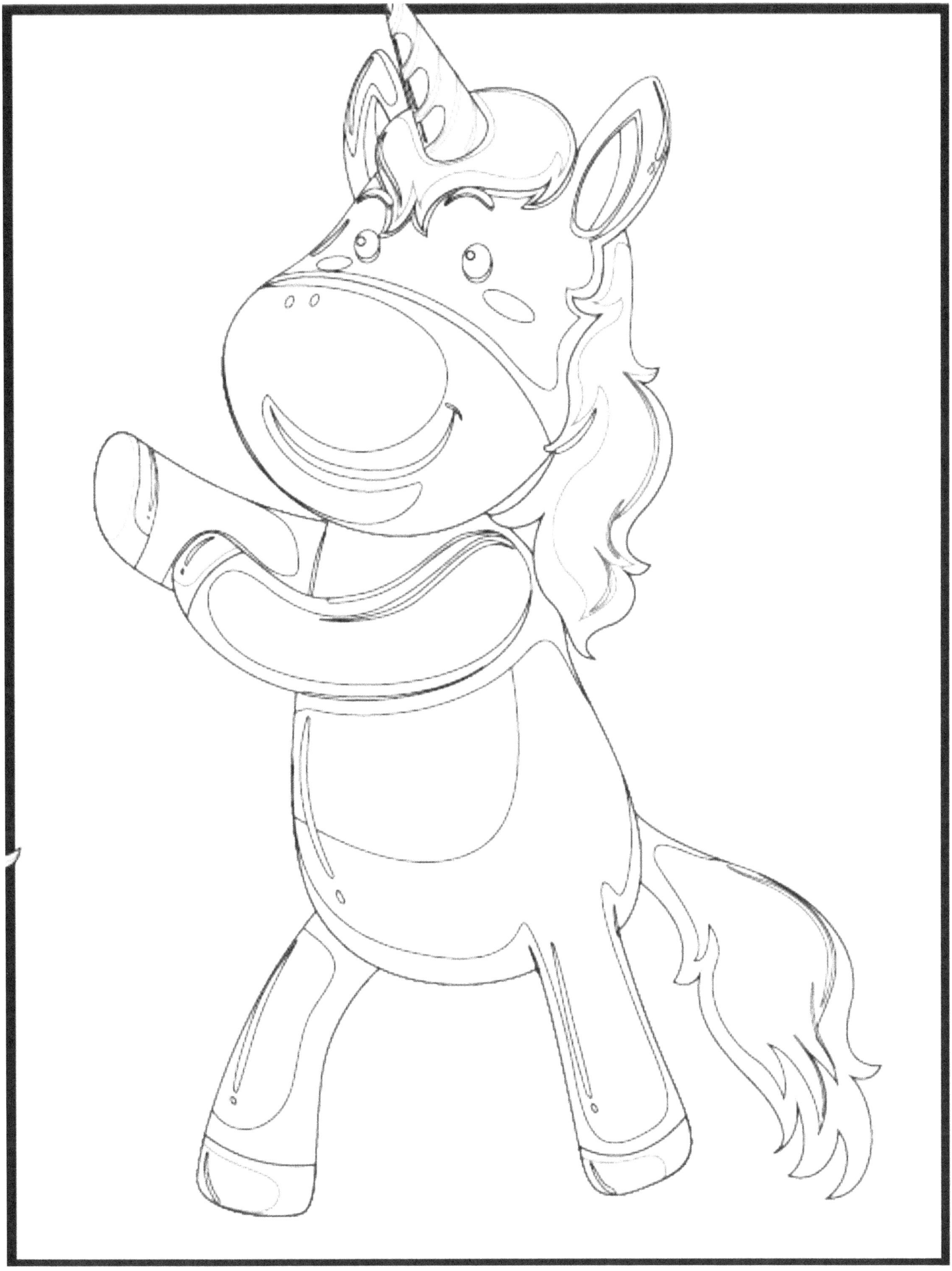

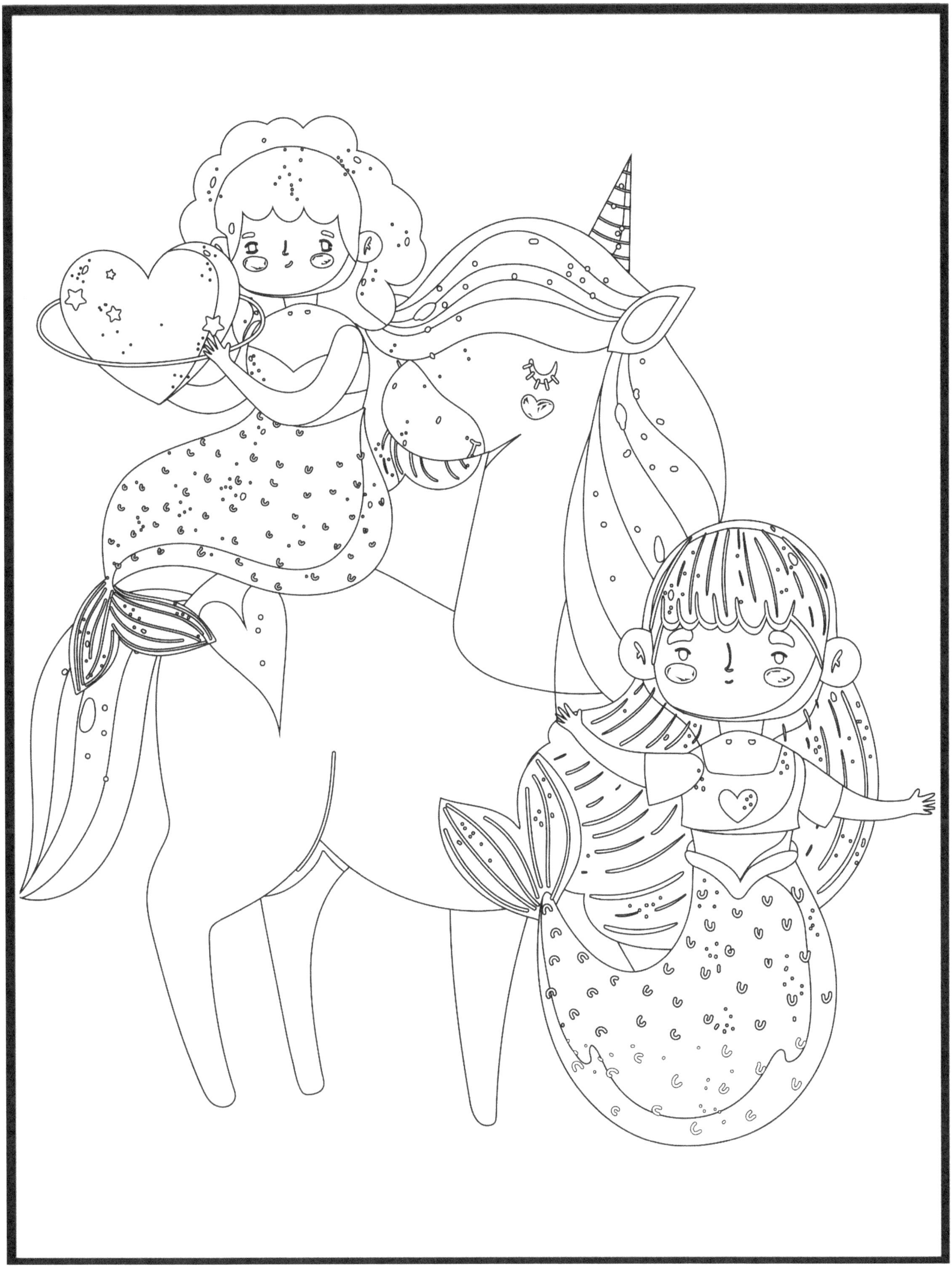

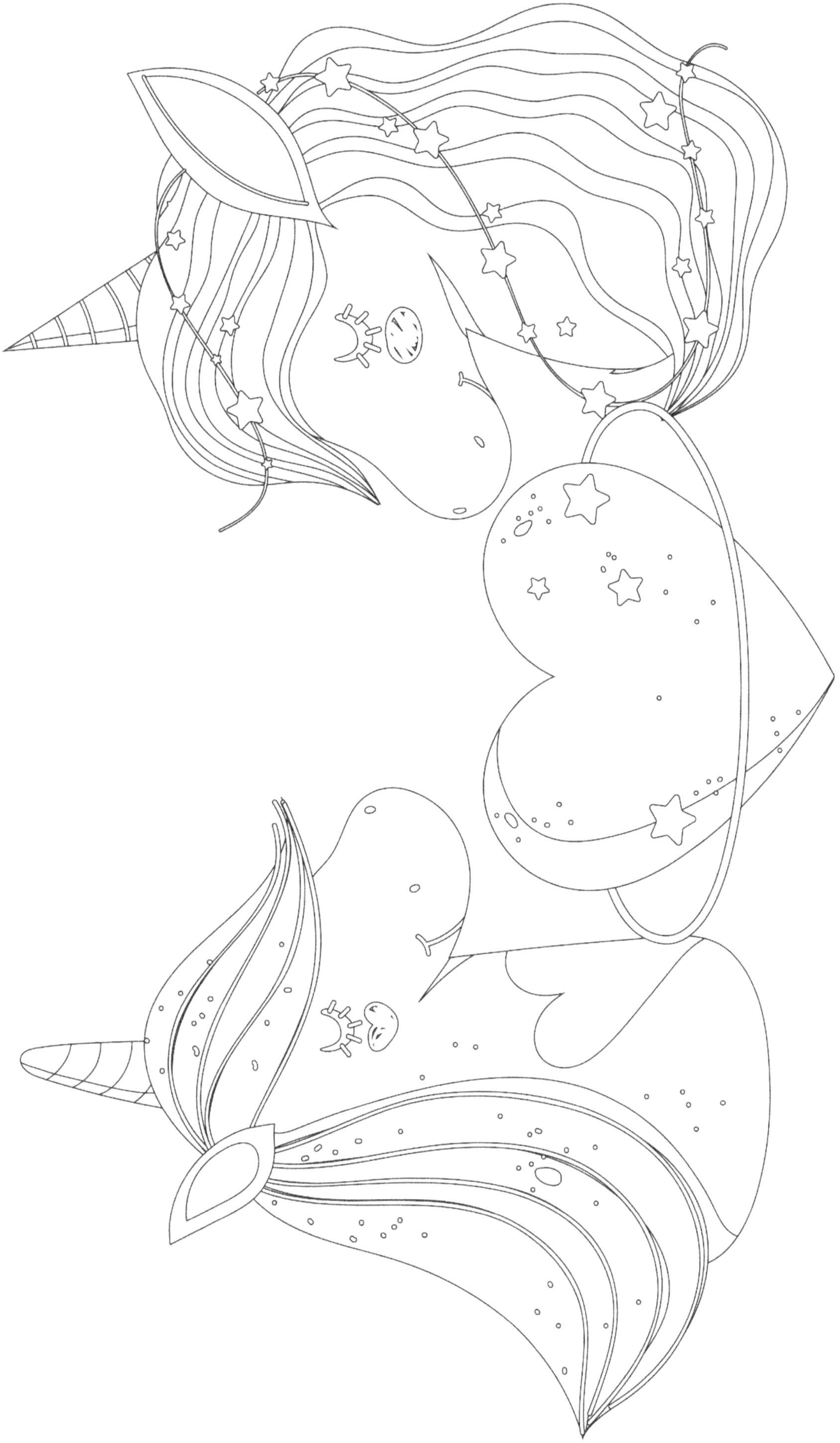

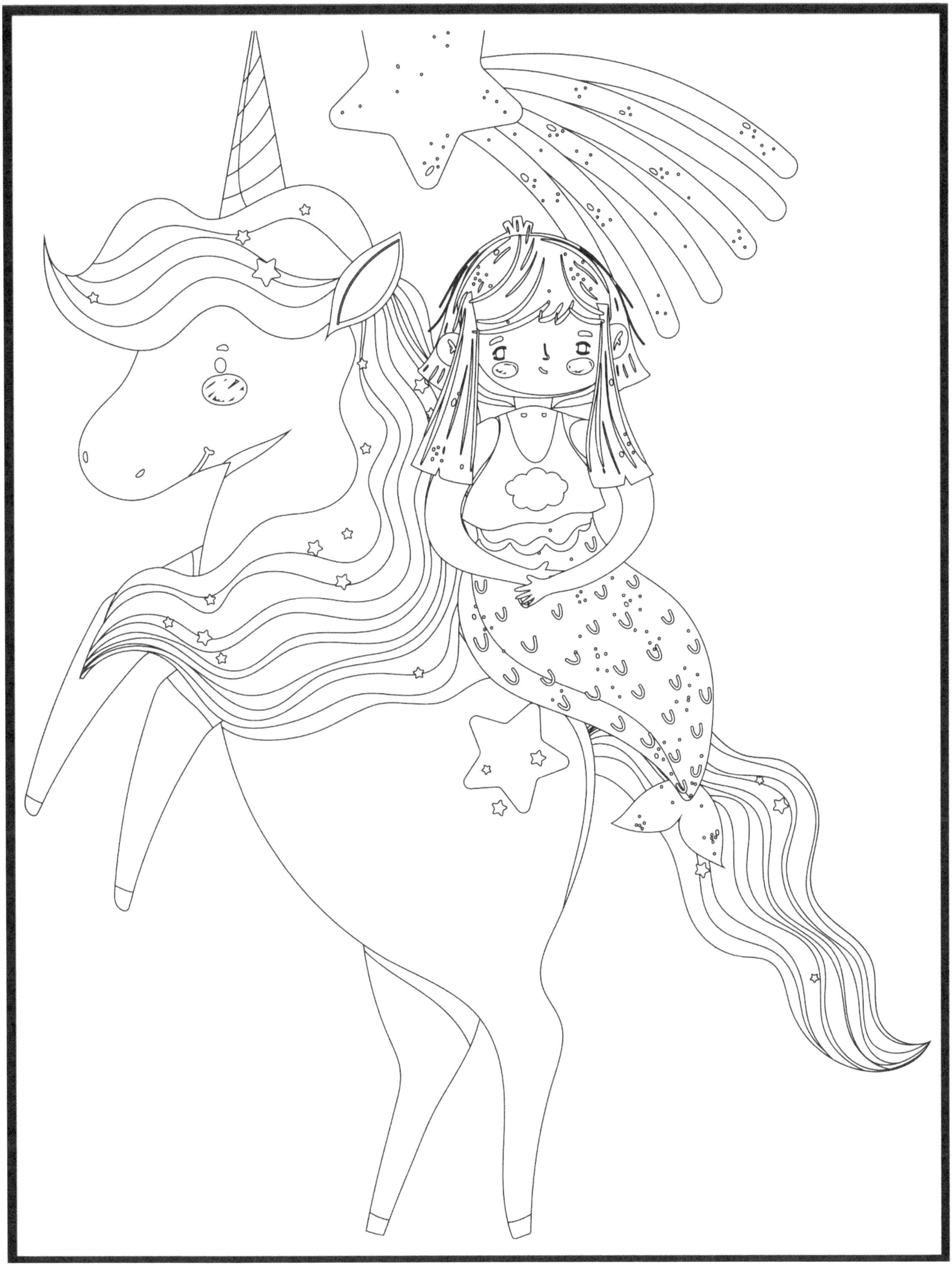

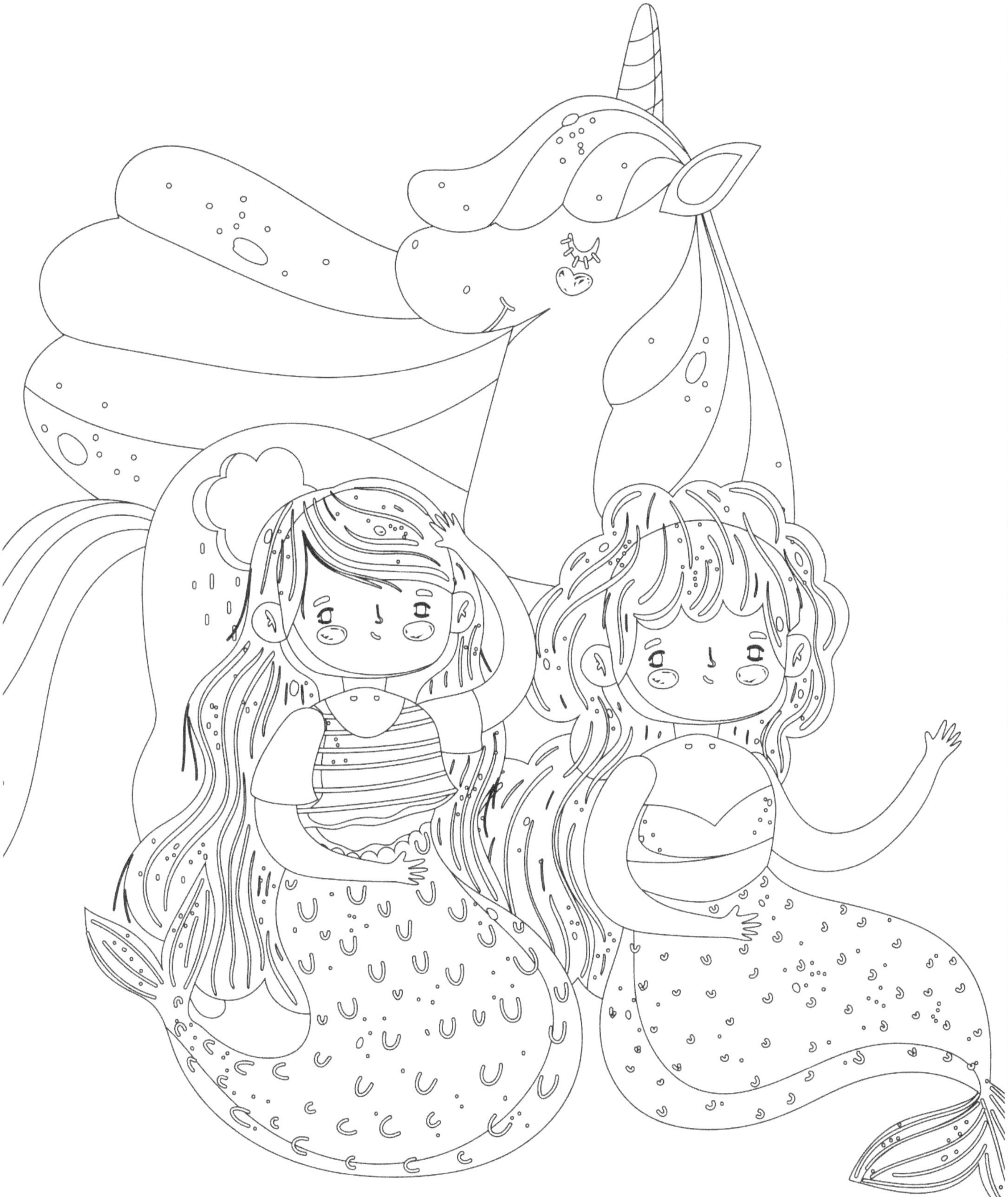

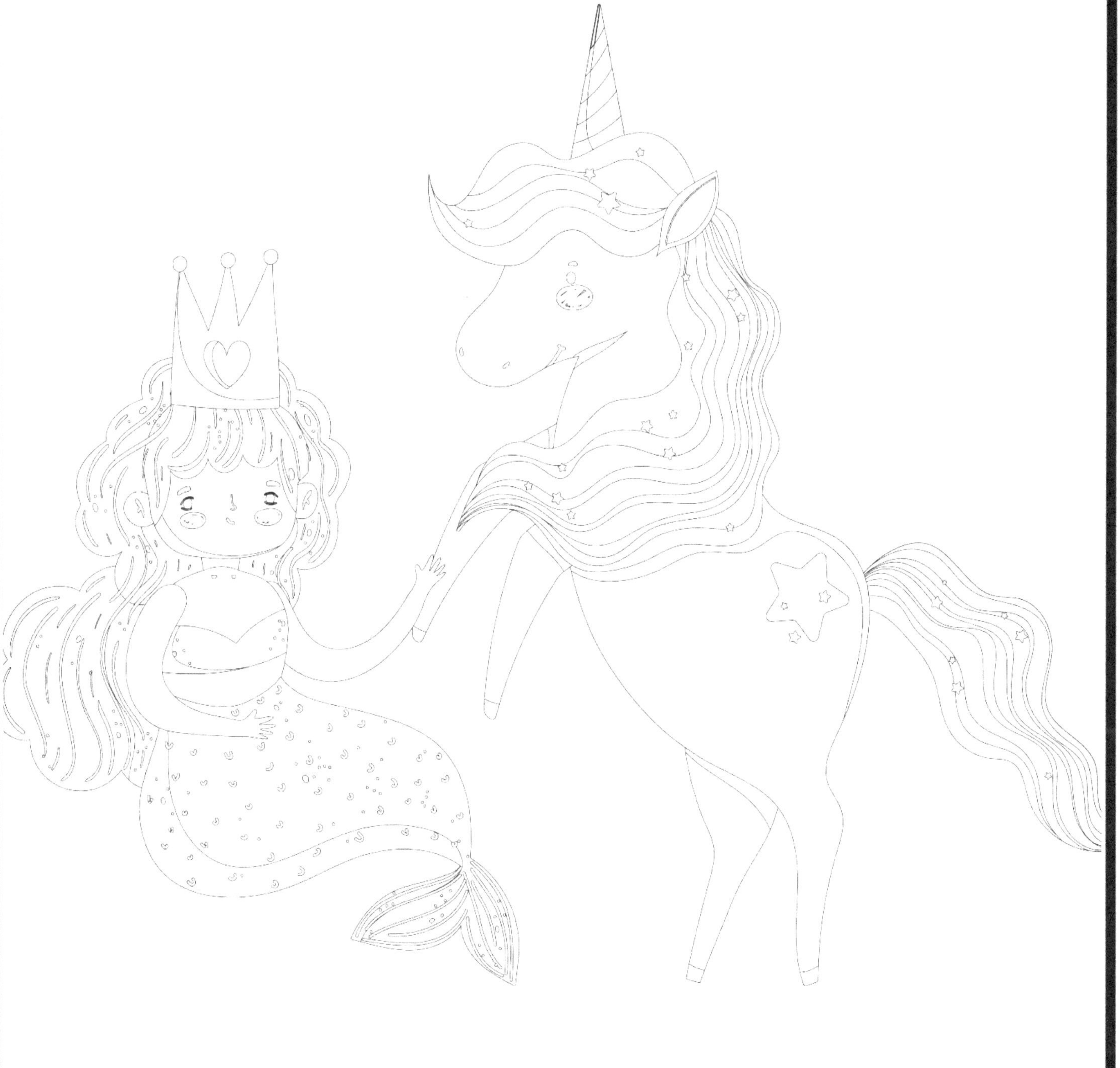

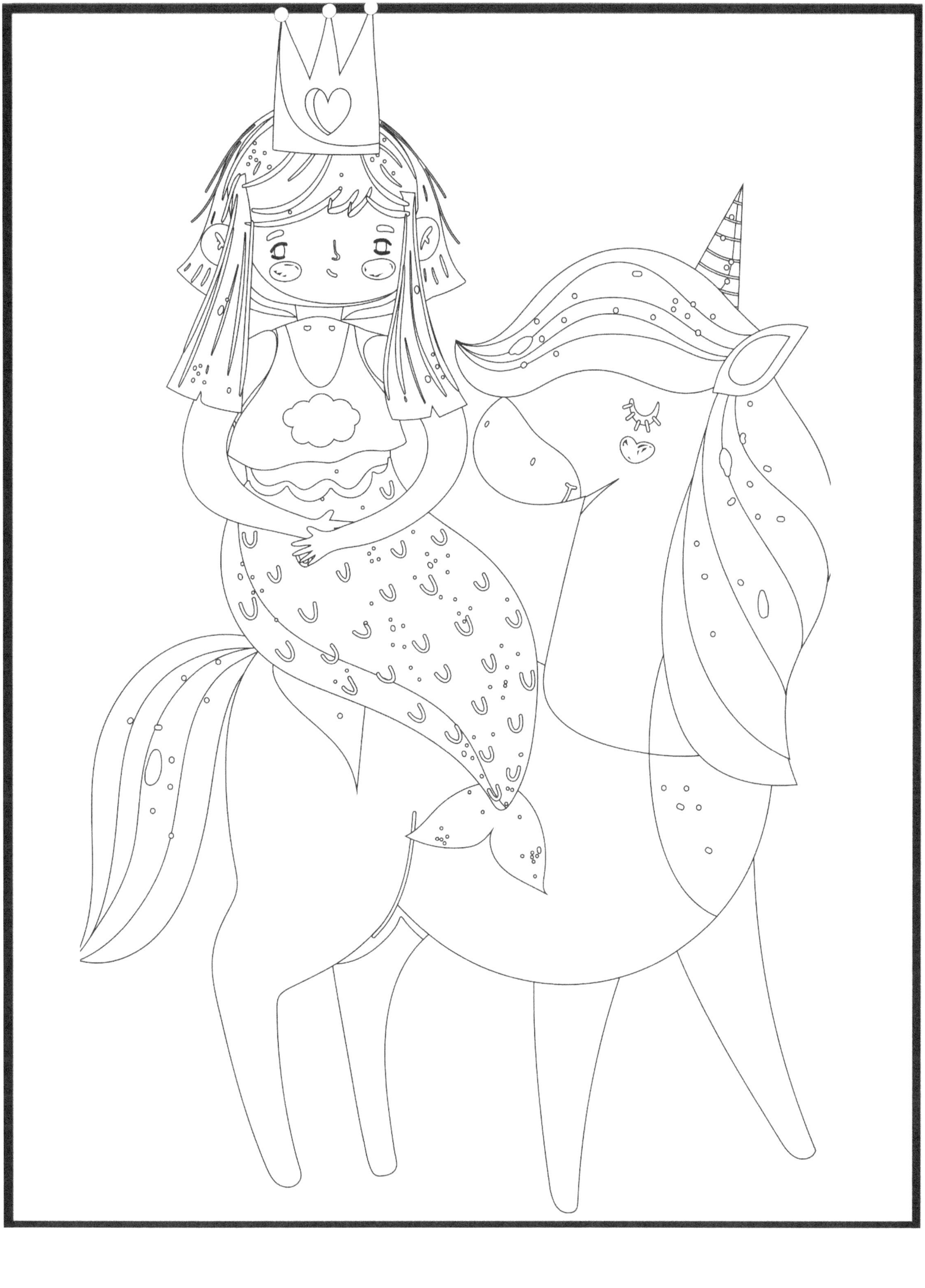

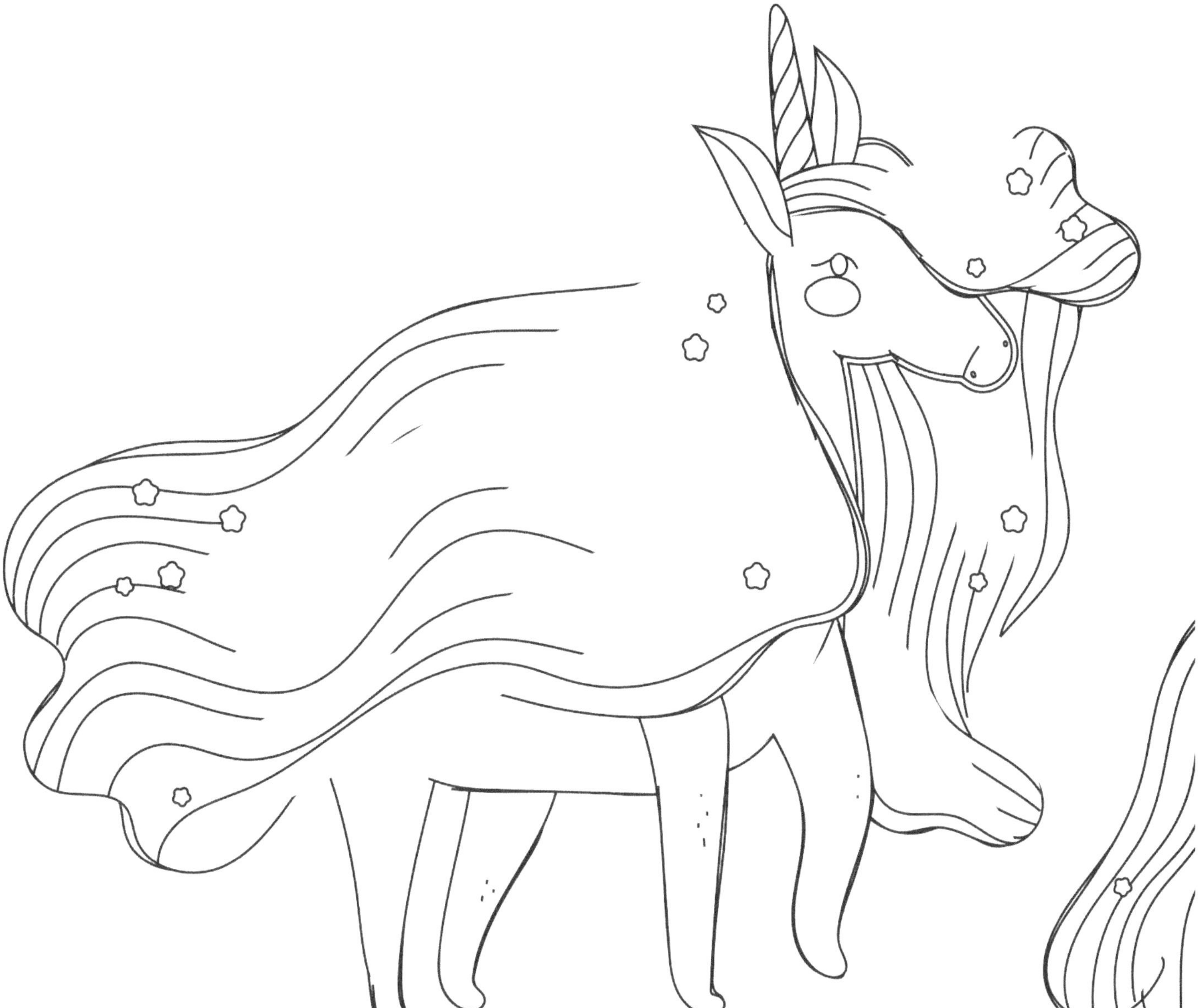

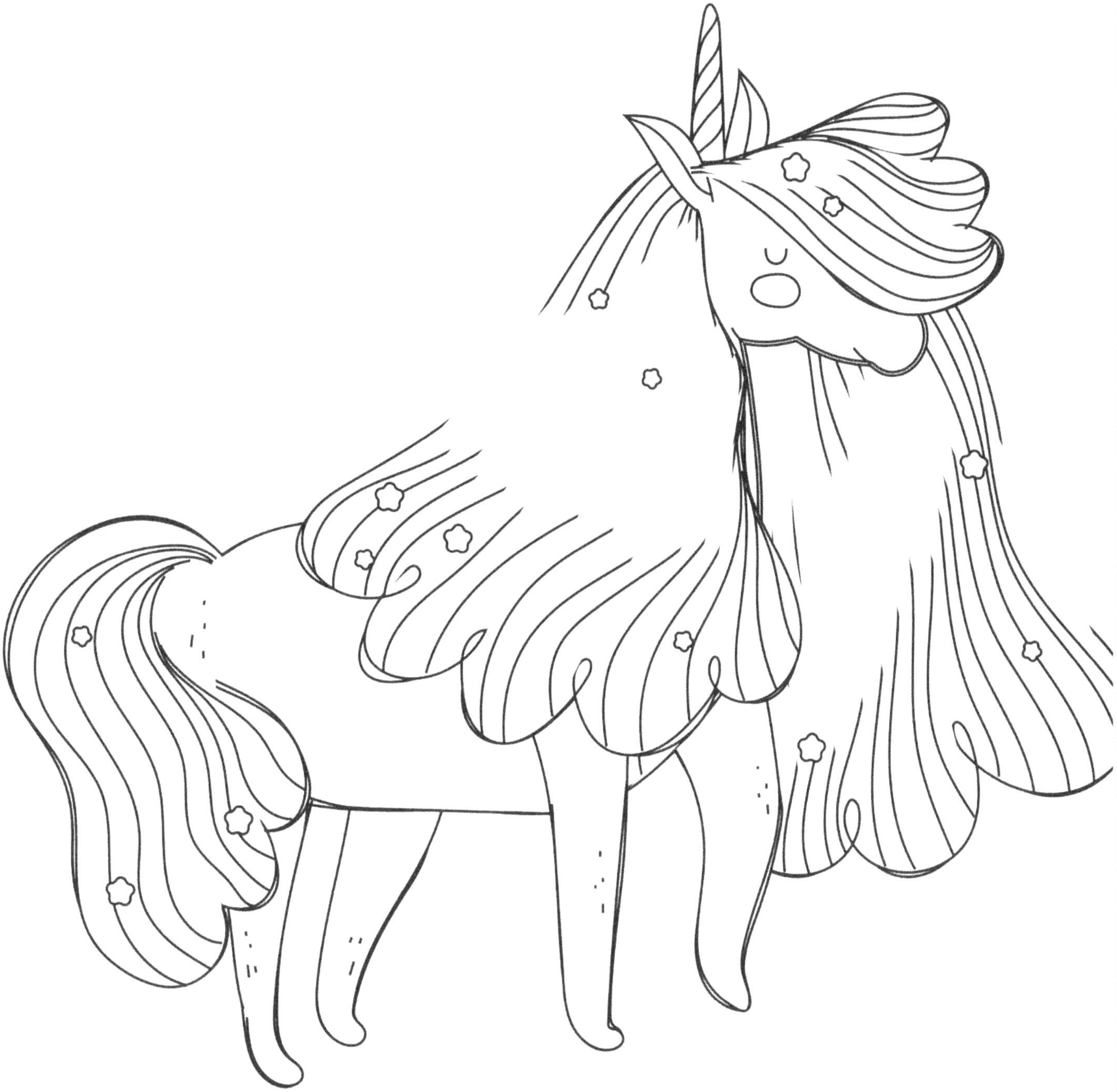

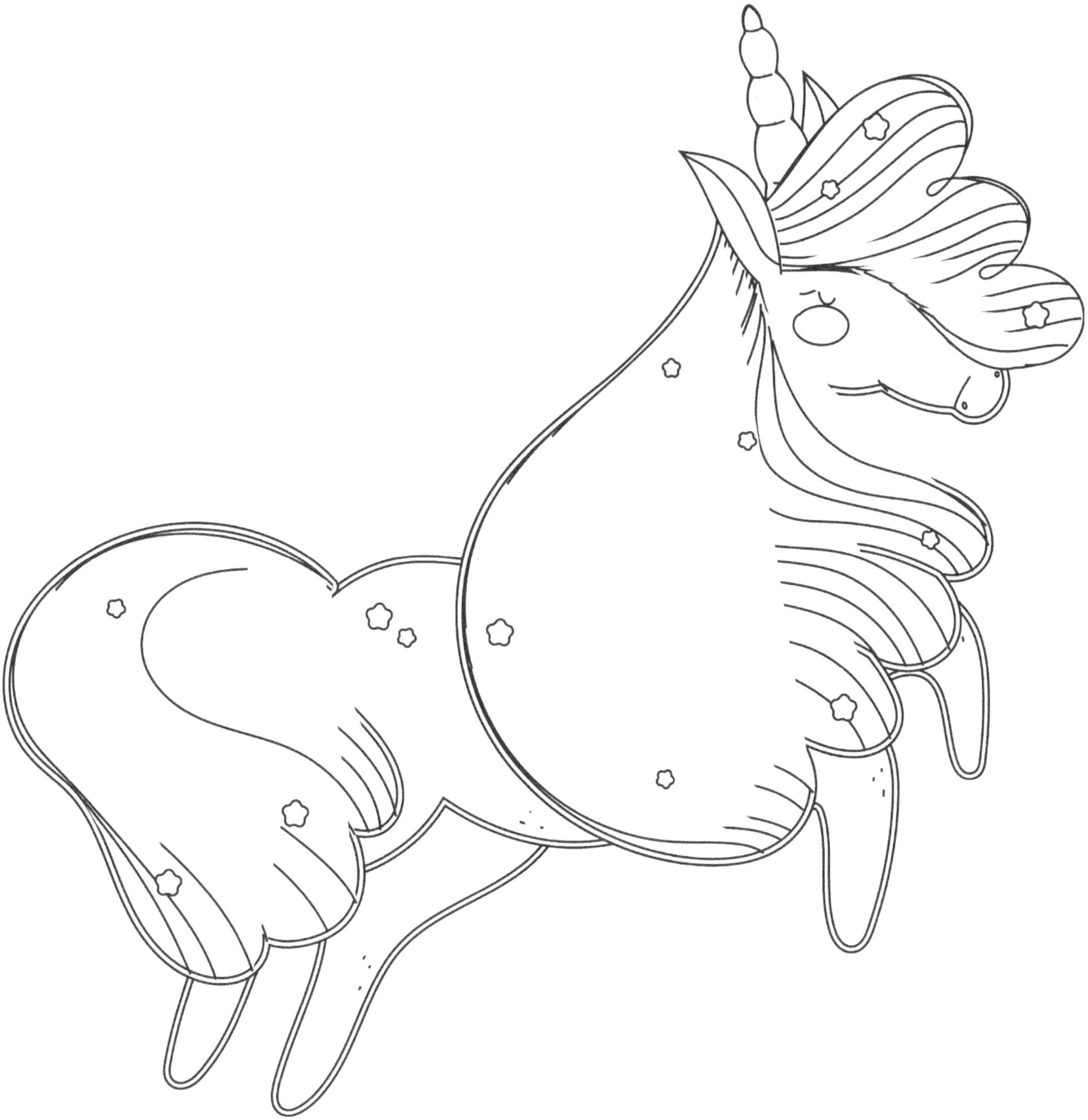

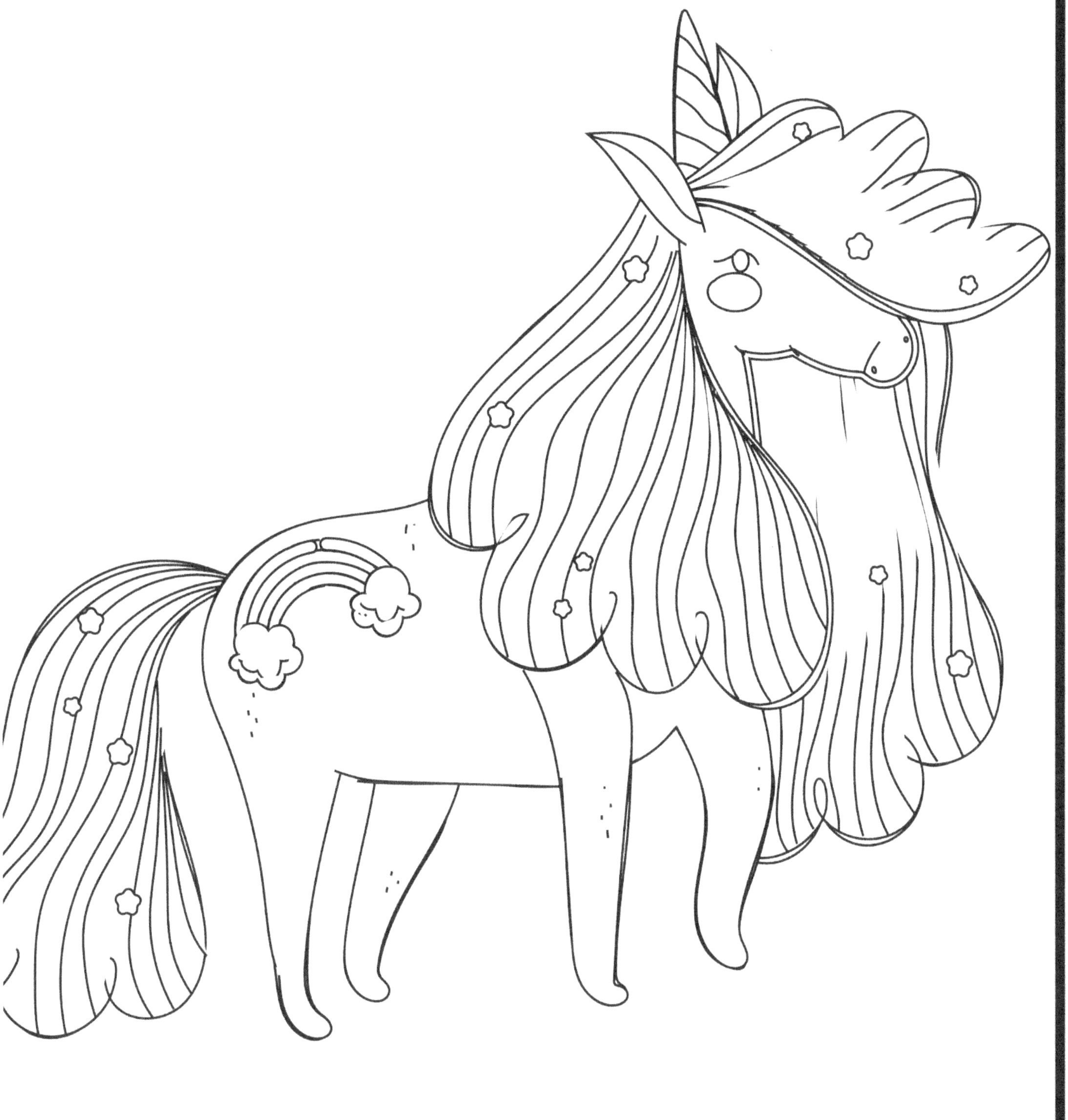

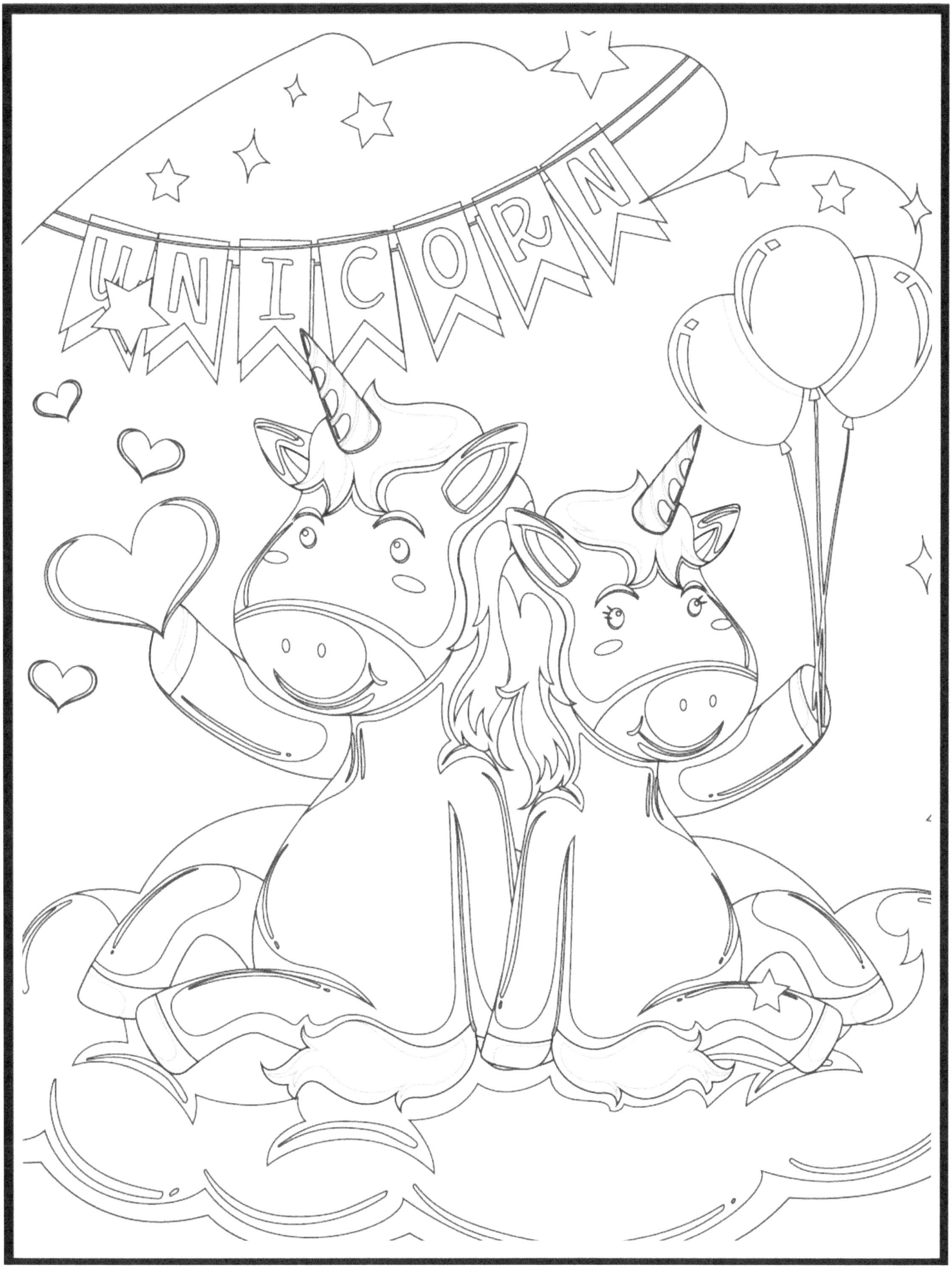
UNICORN

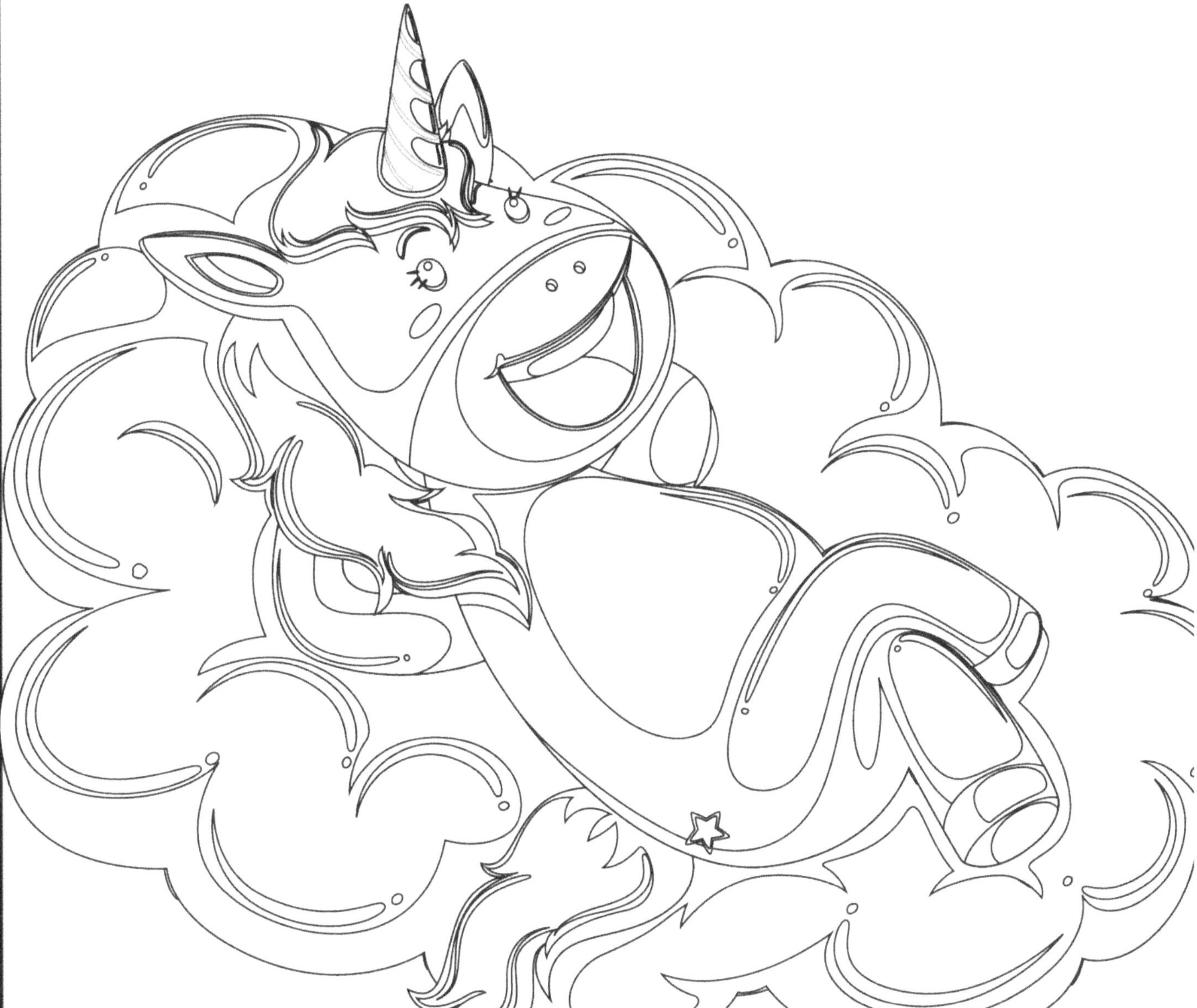

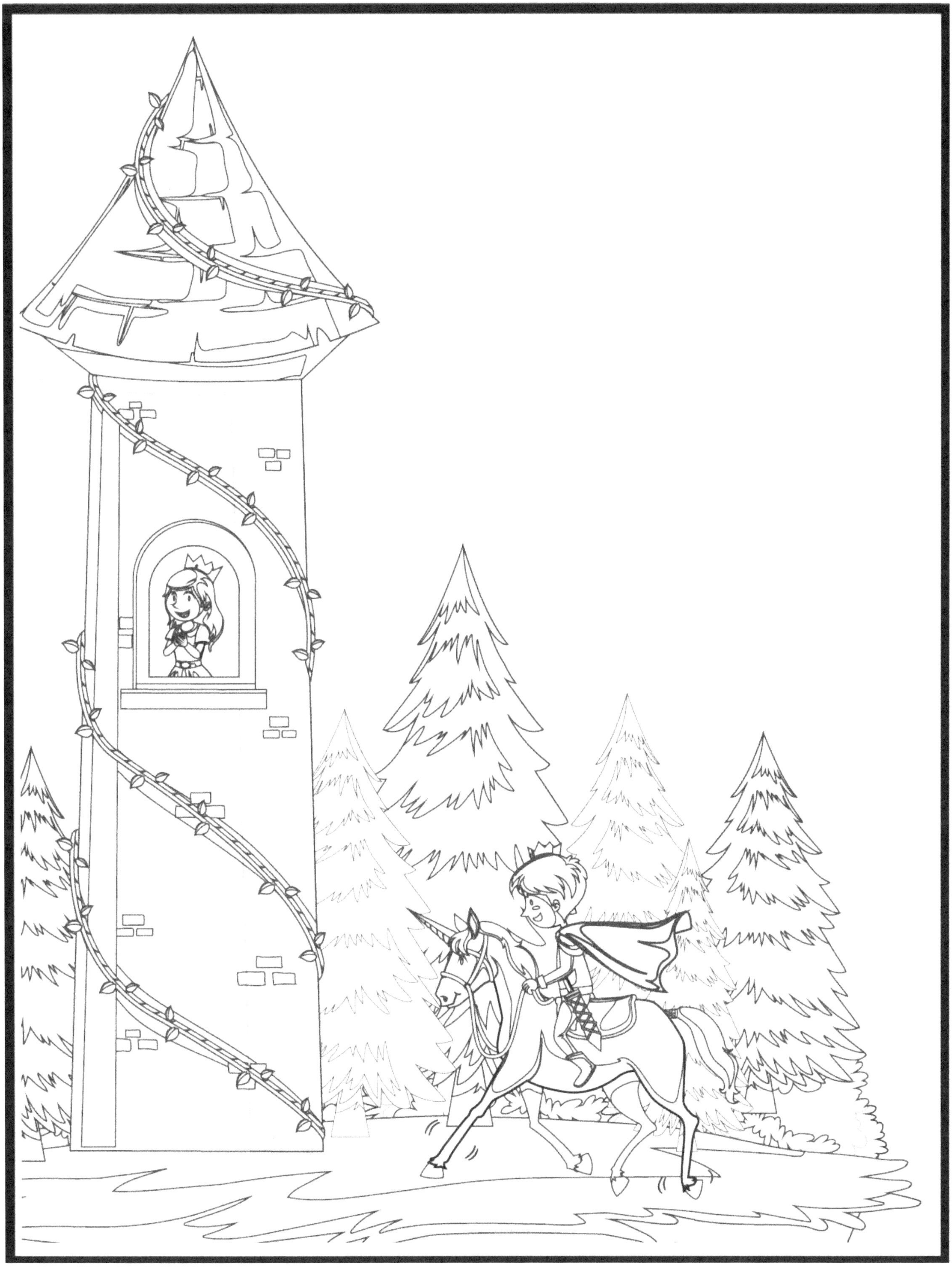

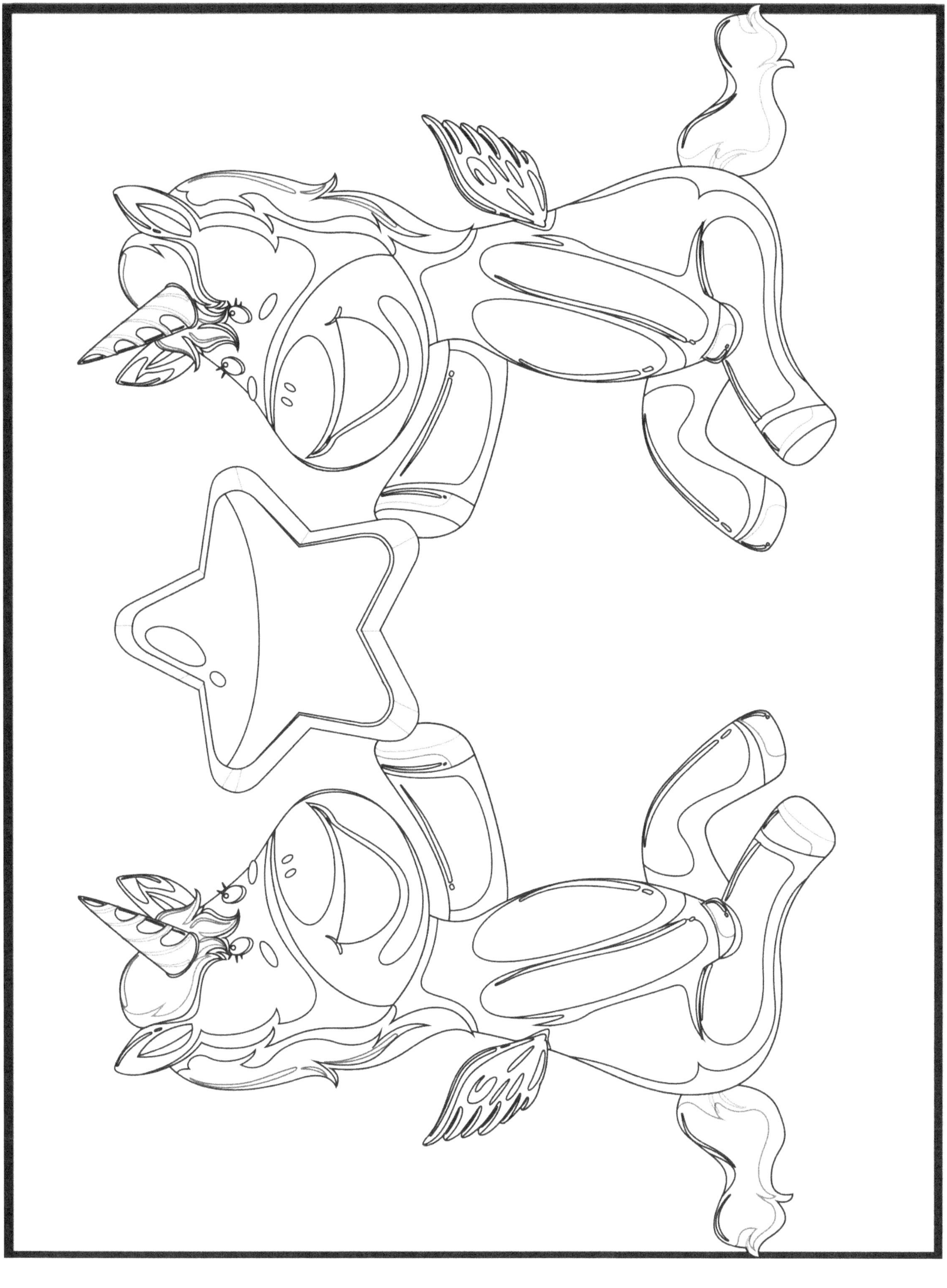

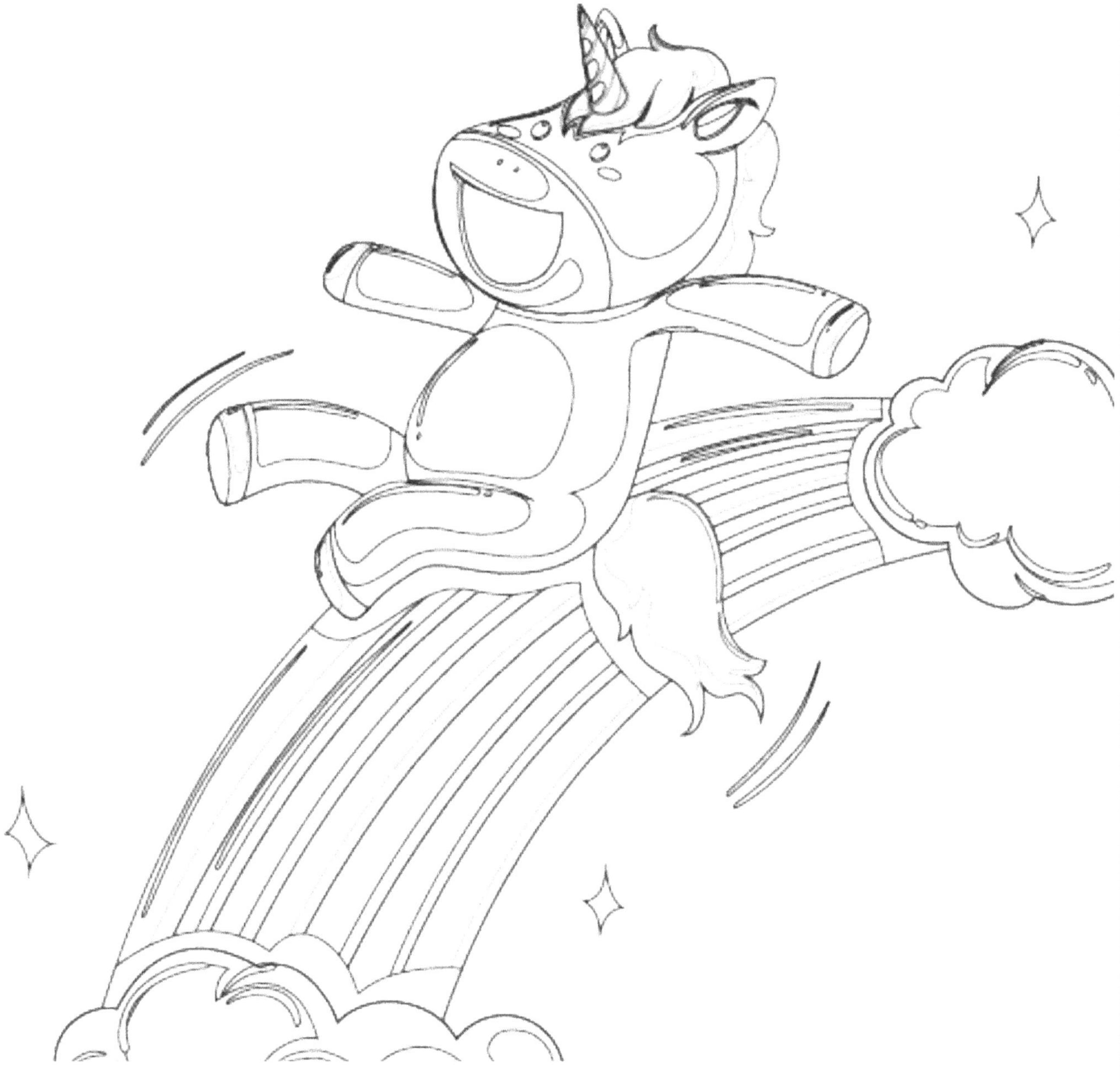

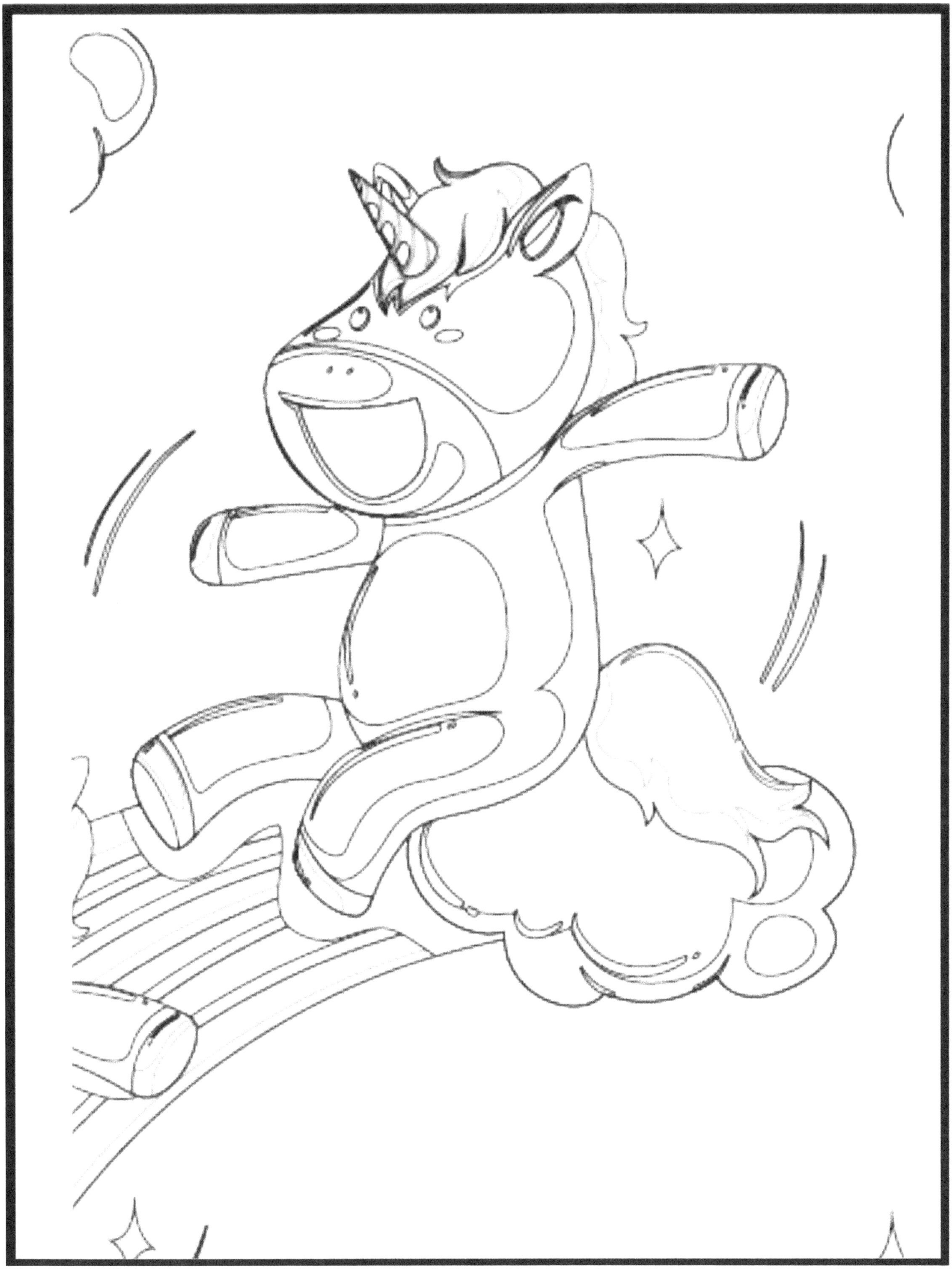

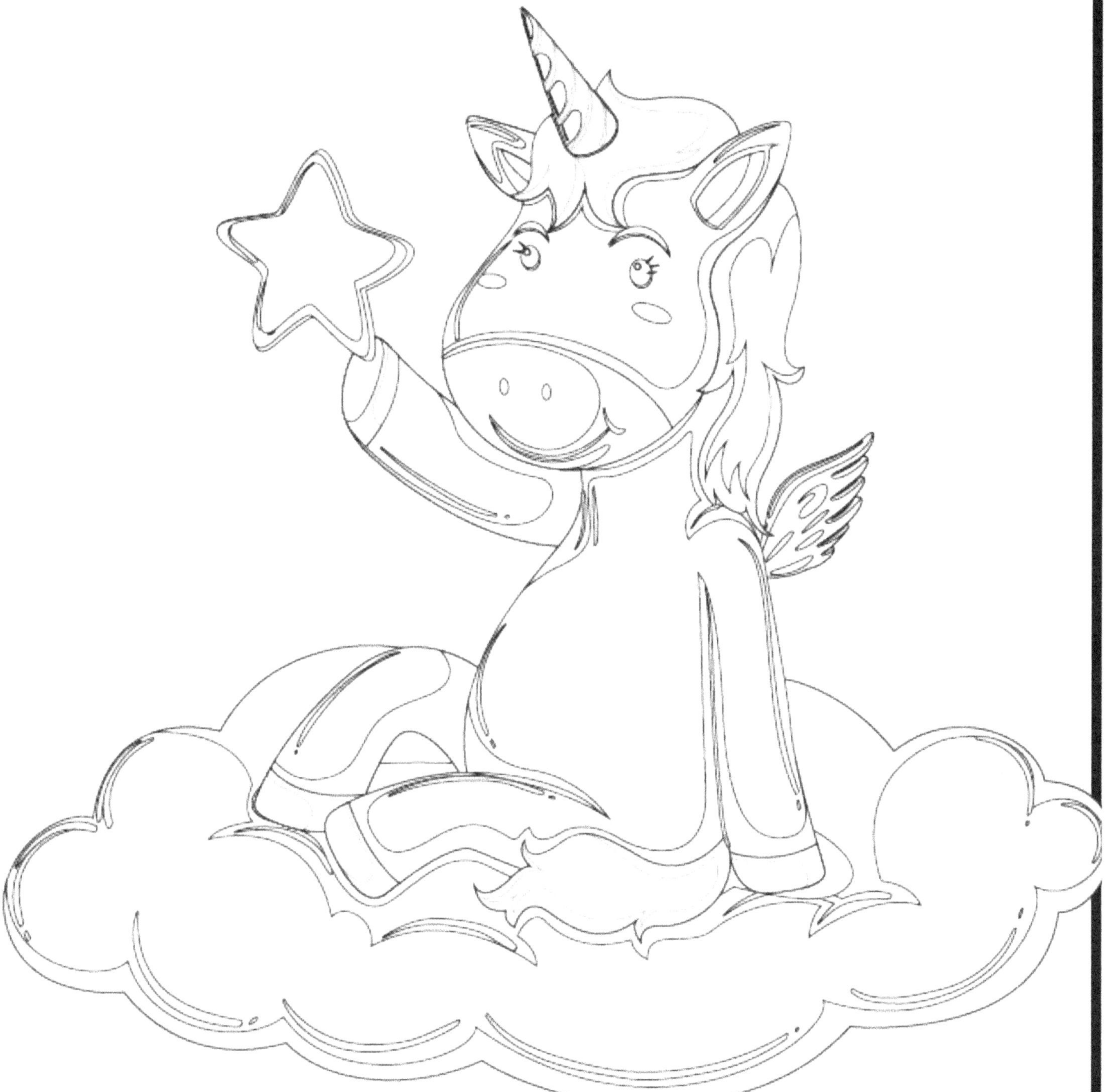

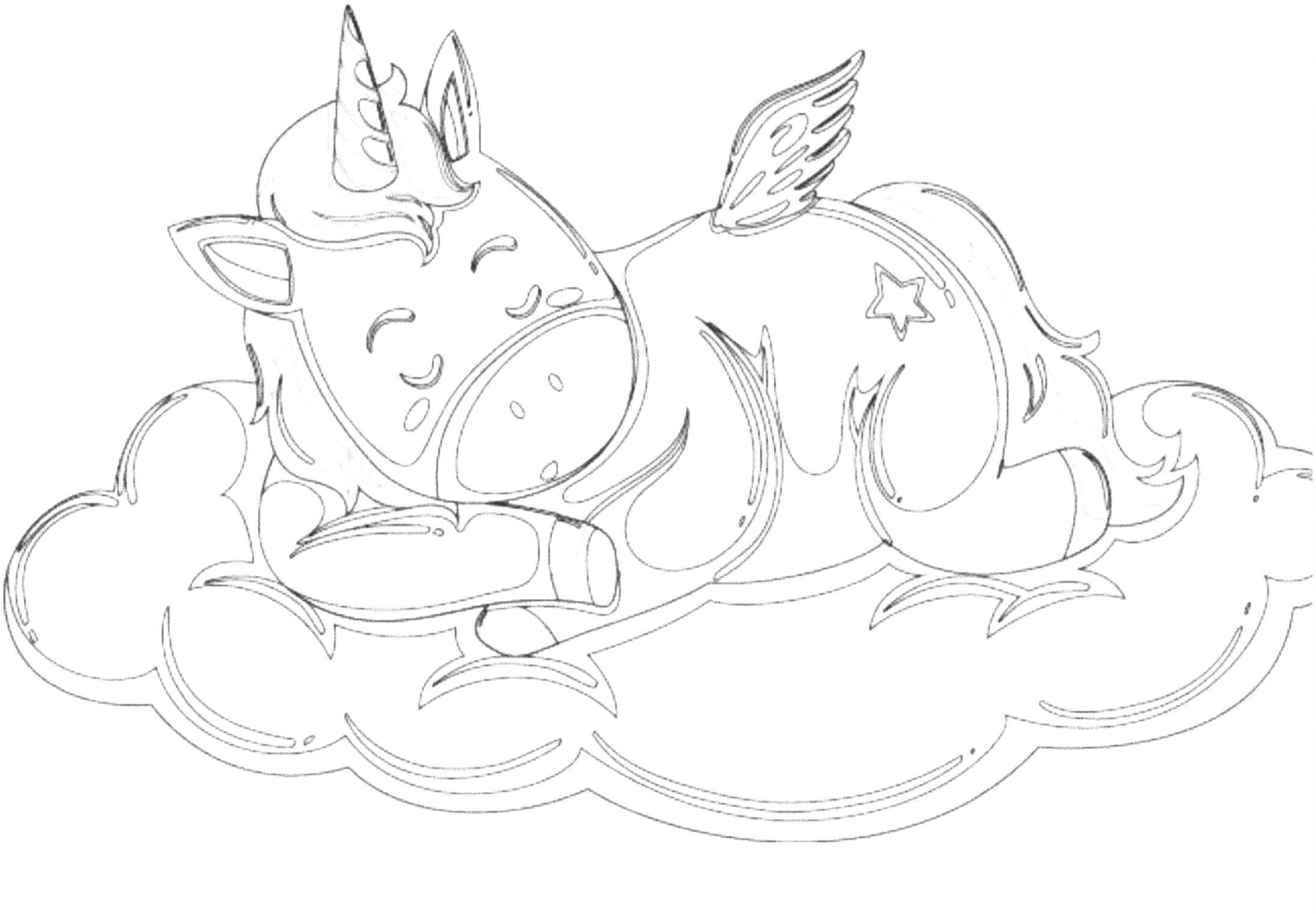

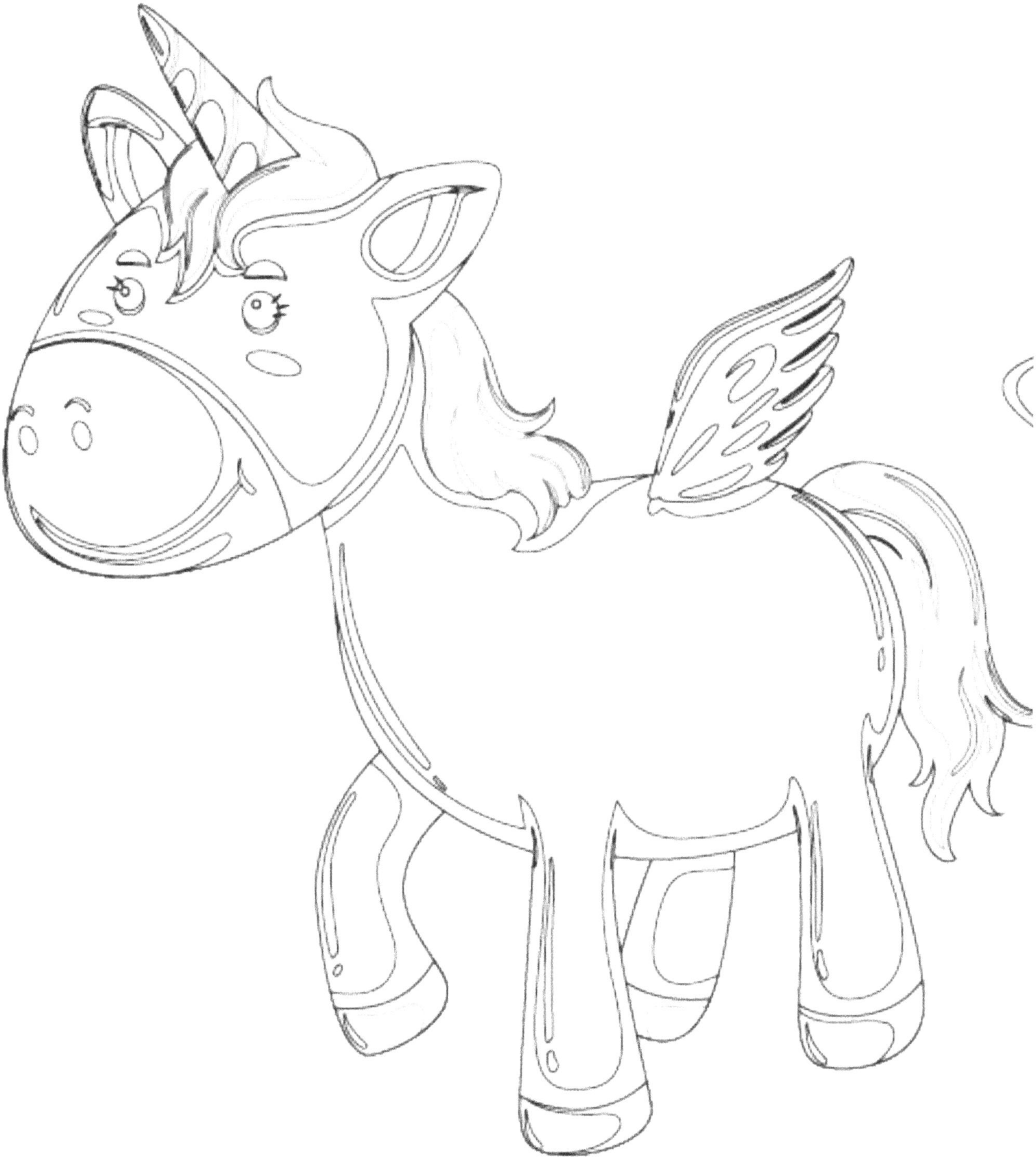

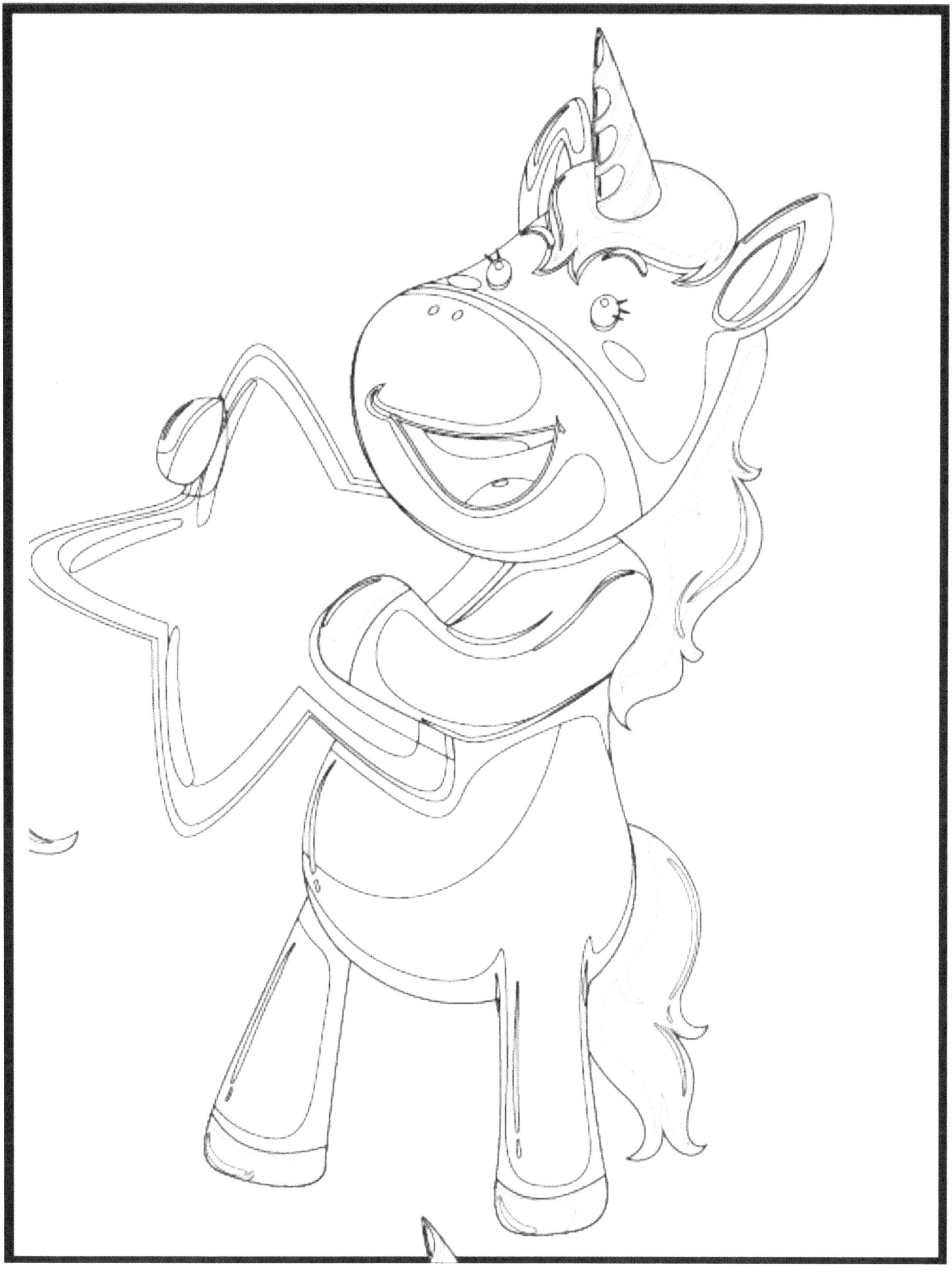

www.ingramcontent.com/pod-product-compliance
Lightning Source LLC
Chambersburg PA
CBHW081058240526
45465CB00025B/2576
9798749765373